Now That's Italian!

Susan Vollmer and Laura Wilson

A Nitty Gritty® Cookbook

Printed in the United States of America.

ISBN 1-55867-069-6

Cover design: Frank Paredes
Cover photographer: John Benson
Food stylist: Suzanne Carreiro
Production consultant: Vicki L. Crampton
Illustrator: Carol Webb Atherly

CONTENTS

TRENTINO-
ALTO ADIGE

FRIULI-VENEZIA
GIULIA

AOSTA VALLEY

VENETO

LOMBARDY

PIEDMONT

Venice

Parma

EMILIA-
ROMAGNA

LIGURIA

Bologna

Genoa

San Marino

TUSCANY

THE
MARCHES

Adriatic Sea

Florence

UMBRIA

*Ligurian
Sea*

ABRUZZI

LATIUM

Rome

MOLISE

CAMPANIA

APULIA

SARDINIA

Naples

BASILI-
CATA

Mediterranean Sea

Salerno

Tyrrhenian Sea

CALABRIA

ITALY

Palermo

SICILY

Introduction

Italian cooking? There is no simple definition. If you have traveled through Italy, you are aware of the tremendous variety of Italian cuisine. Until the unification of Italy in 1861, there were separate and usually hostile city-states, each with its own ruler, customs and culture.

While there are still classic regional foods, Italy is slowly losing its regional diversity. Previously isolated towns are now connected by superhighways. This mobility tends to lessen sharp distinctions.

However, there remain pronounced differences between the Northern and Southern styles of cooking. And each town within a region may claim its own version of a soup or pasta dish.

We can trace some of the distinctions to geography. Northern Italy, the dairy zone, has fertile plains and pastures. Therefore, butter is used in cooking, sauces are mild and creamy, rice and polenta are staples and veal is a specialty. From the Appennines stretching westward to the Adriatic lies the gastronomic region of Emilia-Romagna, with its supreme cooking capital of Bologna. Here is the home of the famous Parmigiano-Reggiano cheese.

In the mountainous, more arid southern portion of the country lie groves of olive trees, so olive oil replaces the butter of the North. The flour and egg pasta of the North changes to an eggless macaroni. Naples and the southward area have more colorful and highly seasoned dishes. The sauces are pungent with ripe tomatoes, oregano, Romano cheese and the occasional addition of red-hot chili peppers. Kid and lamb replace veal as the main meat dish.

Traditional Italian cuisine is changing. The main multi-course meal is served at noon while businesses are closed for several hours. With more women working outside the home, time to spend in the kitchen is becoming scarce. Meals are becoming lighter and are less apt to follow the classic pattern. Meals are usually eaten at home rather than in restaurants. With the italian love of eating, gatherings at the dinner table represent the sharing of food, friendship and sense of family.

We hope your Italian meals will do the same.

Ingredients

To capture the essence and flavor of Italian cooking, you need to know its basic ingredients. The key is in choosing the top-quality fresh ingredients which are used throughout this book. Following is a listing of key ingredients that characterize Italian food and its flavors.

Olive Oils

Olive oil is a fundamental ingredient in Italian cooking in the Central and Southern regions. There are three grades of olive oil. *Extra Virgin Olive Oil* is from the first cold pressing of high-quality, ripe, undamaged olives. It is very green in color and has a wonderfully pungent taste. It is best used sparingly and uncooked in sauces and salads to appreciate its intense flavor. *Virgin Olive Oil* is also from the first cold pressing but the olives are not of top quality. *Pure Olive Oil* is from many pressings of the olives which produce oils which are blended and refined. Pure olive oil is usually a clear gold color and the taste is much lighter than a virgin or extra virgin olive oil.

Cheeses

Parmesan (also called Parmigiano-Reggiano) is one of the finest cheeses. It is produced between April and November in five small provinces of Emilia.

Parmesan is straw yellow in color and has a slightly salty taste. It is superb for cooking. Always buy Parmesan by the piece and grate only when needed. Do not substitute commercially prepacked grated cheese. It will have no flavor whatsoever.

Romano is a hard grating cheese made from sheep's milk (also called Pecorino Romano; pecora is Italian for sheep). It comes from Central and Southern Italy and two islands, Sicily and Sardinia. Romano is sharper and more pungent than Parmesan.

Fontina cheese is made exclusively in the Val d'Aosta region of Northern Italy. It is a semi-soft cheese, pale cream in color, with a sweet flavor. Fontina is excellent used in cooking or as a table cheese.

Gorgonzola is a blue cheese made from whole milk and the addition of a harmless fungus. It originated in the town of the same name but is found throughout Italy today. When young, Gorgonzola has a delicate, buttery taste, but the more aged cheese has a pungent, sharp taste. It is used as a dessert cheese with fresh fruit (especially pears) and in sauces.

Ricotta is made with cow's and sheep's milk. It is a soft, white milk product made from whey, the watery part of milk which separates from the curd. Ricotta is sweeter and moister than cottage cheese. It is used in many cooked dishes as well as in desserts.

Mozzarella is best made from water buffalo's milk but is also made from cow's milk. Good mozzarella should be white and elastic and retain its moistness when sliced. As it melts it turns stringy. It is eaten as is, in a salad with tomatoes and fresh basil, breaded and deep-fried or melted in dishes.

Tomatoes

A tomato vine-ripened by the heat of the summer sun has no equal when used in sauces and salads. The best tomatoes are the long, narrow plump ones.

When fresh tomatoes are not available use the "San Marzano" canned plum tomatoes. These deep red, ripe and flavorful peeled tomatoes are hand-picked in the Salerno province of Southern Italy.

Air-dried tomatoes and dried tomatoes preserved in oil are making an appearance in markets. A paste is derived from this product for adding to dishes in small quantities.

Pancetta

Pancetta is an Italian bacon used as a flavoring. It is cured in salt and spices rather than smoked. You will find pancetta in Italian markets, shaped like a salami and sliced to order. There is no exact substitute for pancetta but prosciutto or unsmoked ham will do when it is unobtainable.

Prosciutto

Prosciutto is an unsmoked, salted and air-cured ham. Prosciutto is also found in Italian markets and is quite expensive.

Here is a list of the main herbs used in Italian cooking:

Basil — used to flavor dishes in Northern Italy. It is the king of the aromatic herbs. Fresh picked basil has a refreshing and distinctive quality which can liven the simplest of dishes. Dried basil is no substitute for fresh.

Bay Leaves — go well with braised meats.

Marjoram — used in soups and meat dishes in Northern and Central Italy.

Oregano — used in Southern Italy to flavor tomato sauces.

Rosemary — used to flavor meat and poultry dishes.

Sage — goes particularly well with veal, game and roasted potatoes.

Appetizers

The Italian word "antipasto" literally translated means "before the pasta." All of these antipasti are meant to be served before the meal. However, an appetizer course is not usually served as part of an Italian family meal. It is more often served with formal meals and parties. If at home, simple appetizers such as prosciutto wrapped around fresh melon make a wonderful combination.

The best setting for antipasti is in a restaurant where samples are presented and displayed to entice every arriving customer. Italians have the belief that you eat first with your eyes, and then with your palate.

We've included in this chapter some appetizers that could be part of a family meal as well as others that could well be a lovely addition to a party.

APPETIZERS

Roasted Peppers
with Basil and Mozzarella

Servings: 6

Bright layers of red pepper, white mozzarella and green basil make a beautiful and delicious appetizer.

6 red bell peppers
½ lb. mozzarella cheese, sliced
12 fresh basil leaves
½ cup olive oil

4 garlic cloves, minced
2 tbs. chopped fresh basil
salt and freshly ground pepper to taste

Roast peppers under the broiler until the skin is dark brown and blistered. Place in a plastic bag and set aside for 10 minutes. Peel and clean peppers. Cut into large strips and pat dry with paper towels. On a large platter, arrange peppers and cheese in slightly overlapping layers. Place basil leaves between the layers. In a small bowl, combine oil, garlic, basil, salt and pepper. Spoon dressing over peppers and cheese. Refrigerate for 1-2 hours. Serve at room temperature.

Fried Cheese with Red Sauce

Servings: 6

A golden crust enveloping melted cheese is presented on a bed of bright red Italian sauce. Remember to have the cheese very cold before you begin frying.

6 (1 oz. each) slices mozzarella or
   provolone cheese, cut ¾" thick
3 eggs
2 cups milk
salt and pepper

1 tbs. chopped fresh parsley
3 cups bread crumbs
3 cups flour
Red Sauce
garnish: chopped fresh parsley

In a large bowl combine eggs, milk, salt, pepper and parsley and mix well. Place the bread crumbs and flour on separate plates. Dip a cheese slice into the egg mixture, then into the flour, then into the egg, and finally into the flour again. Dip into the egg one last time and then roll in bread crumbs. Refrigerate until ready to cook. Heat vegetable oil in a deep fat fryer or saucepan to 375°. Fry cheese until golden brown. Serve immediately with red sauce. Sprinkle chopped parsley on top.

Red Sauce

¼ cup butter
¼ cup olive oil
1 onion, finely chopped
1 bell pepper, finely chopped
3 garlic cloves, minced
2 tsp. oregano
½ cup red wine
1 (28 ozs.) can Italian plum tomatoes

Place butter and olive oil in a large skillet over medium heat. When butter has melted, add onion, pepper, and garlic. Sauté for about 10 minutes. Add the remaining ingredients and simmer for about 20 minutes until sauce is thickened.

Mushrooms Stuffed with Spinach and Prosciutto

Servings: 7-12

This pound of fresh mushrooms will give you 14 to 24 mushrooms (depending on size) with a delicious stuffing of spinach and prosciutto.

1 lb. large mushrooms
2 tsp. olive oil
salt and freshly ground
   pepper to taste
4 tsp. fresh lemon juice
1 tbs. butter
¼ cup minced onion
1 (10 ozs.) pkg. frozen chopped
   spinach, thawed

2 tbs. heavy cream
⅛ tsp. nutmeg
salt and freshly ground pepper to taste
1 egg, lightly beaten
¼ cup minced prosciutto (or other ham)
1 tbs. freshly grated Parmesan cheese

Rinse and dry mushrooms. Remove stems and finely chop them. Set chopped stems aside. Place mushroom caps, stem side down, in a buttered baking dish. Sprinkle with olive oil, salt, pepper and 2 tsp. of lemon juice. Bake in a 400° oven for 5 minutes. Heat butter in a saucepan over medium heat. Add onion and cook about 5 minutes. Add chopped mushroom stems and the remaining 2 tsp. of lemon juice. Cook 1-2 minutes. Add spinach and cook until liquid has evaporated. Add cream, nutmeg, salt and pepper. Add egg and cook about 15 seconds. Spoon the spinach mixture into a food processor or blender. Blend thoroughly. Return to the saucepan and stir in prosciutto. Fill mushroom caps with stuffing. Place, filled side up, on a baking dish. Sprinkle with Parmesan cheese. Bake in a 400° oven for about 12 minutes or until tops are lightly browned.

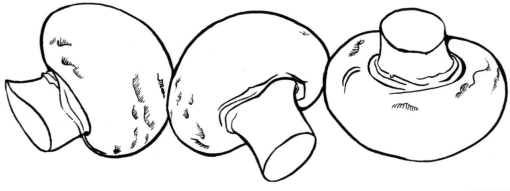

Caponata

A cold Sicilian salad is made of eggplant, celery, tomatoes and other vegetables plus capers, olives and vinegar. This is a marvelous addition to an antipasto.

1 medium eggplant
¼ cup olive oil
1 large onion, chopped
¾ cup celery, sliced
1 bell pepper (red or green),
   cut in chunks
2 cloves garlic, chopped
1¼ lb. tomatoes, peeled,
   seeded and diced
¼ cup red wine vinegar

1 tbs. salt, or to taste
1 tbs. sugar
3 tbs. fresh basil, chopped (or 1 tbs. dried)
2 tbs. tomato paste
1 tsp. freshly ground pepper
⅓ cup sliced stuffed green olives
2 tbs. capers, drained
1 carrot, thinly sliced
1 or 2 zucchini, sliced

Cut unpeeled eggplant into 1" cubes. Heat olive oil in a large saucepan or Dutch oven over medium heat. Add eggplant and onion. Sauté for 5 minutes until lightly golden. Add remaining ingredients, stir thoroughly and simmer (covered) for 30 minutes. Remove lid and simmer 10 minutes more to thicken. Serve at room temperature, in a bowl, surrounded by sliced Italian bread, or as a salad on romaine or as part of any antipasto. Caponata will keep, under refrigeration, for 3 weeks.

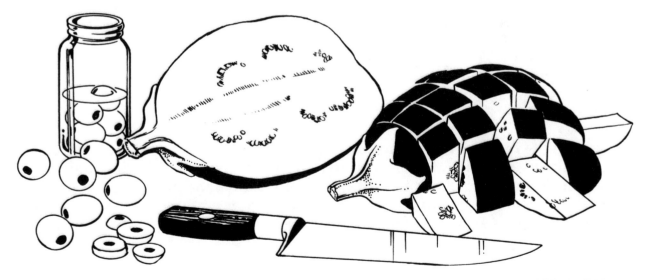

Marinated Sole with Pignoli

This chilled fish is marvelous as another centerpiece of an antipasto.

2 lbs. sole fillets, cut in 2" squares
¾ cup flour
6 tbs. olive oil
salt and freshly ground pepper to taste
1 red onion, thinly sliced
1 cup white wine
½ cup balsamic vinegar
¼ cup pine nuts (pignoli)
¼ cup raisins

Dredge sole in flour. Heat 4 tbs. olive oil in a large skillet over medium heat. Lightly brown fish. Season with salt and pepper. Transfer to a baking dish. Heat remaining 2 tbs. oil in the same skillet over medium heat. Add onion and sauté about 10 minutes. Do not brown onion. Stir in remaining ingredients and simmer 5 minutes. Pour over fish, cover and refrigerate for 3-4 hours. Serve on a platter.

Stuffed Artichokes

A spicy stuffing is used to accent the delicate flavor of artichokes.

2 large artichokes
fresh lemons
Stuffing

1⅓ cups bread crumbs
1½ tbs. minced garlic
¼ cup minced parsley
½ cup grated Parmesan cheese
4 anchovy fillets, finely chopped
1½ tbs. lemon juice

1 tsp. basil
½ tsp. rosemary
1 tsp. salt
½ tsp. black pepper
¼ cup olive oil
garnish: olive oil, 2 lemon slices

Cut off about one-half inch from the top of each artichoke. Cut off the tip of each leaf. Slice off the stem. Remove the fuzzy choke. Squeeze lemon juice over the cut surfaces. In a large bowl combine stuffing ingredients and mix well. Fill the center of each artichoke with stuffing, as well as the base of each leaf. Drizzle tops with olive oil. Top each with a slice of lemon. Pour about 1-2 inches of water into a Dutch oven. Lightly salt the water. Place the artichokes in the pan and simmer about 45-50 minutes or until a leaf can be pulled easily from the artichoke.

Salmon Mousse

Salmon is blended with olive oil, lemon juice and whipped cream for a light appetizer that is excellent served on crackers.

1 (15 ozs.) can salmon
¼ cup olive oil
2 tbs. fresh lemon juice
⅛ tsp. salt
freshly ground pepper to taste
1½ cups whipping cream (well chilled)

Drain salmon and remove any bones and skin. Crumble it into a blender. Add oil, lemon juice, salt and pepper. Blend until smooth. Spoon into a serving bowl. In a cold mixing bowl, whip cream with an electric mixer until stiff. Fold cream into salmon mixture until completely mixed. Refrigerate for 2 hours before serving. Serve on crackers.

Spicy Shrimp Crostini

Crostini (toasted bread with toppings) in the coastal seaports are most likely to be topped with seafood. Use the red hot pepper according to taste.

1 lb. small shrimp,
   shelled and deveined
¼ cup olive oil
3 garlic cloves, minced
½ to 1 hot red chile pepper, minced

2 tbs. chopped parsley
¾ cup dry white wine
1 cup canned Italian plum tomatoes
¼ cup seasoned bread crumbs
loaf of Italian bread, sliced and broiled

If shrimp are not small ones, cut them into pieces. Heat oil in a large skillet over medium heat. Add garlic, hot chile pepper and parsley. Sauté 60 seconds. Add shrimp and cook for 1 minute. Add wine and cook another minute or until shrimp have just turned pink. Transfer shrimp to bowl. Add tomatoes and bread crumbs to wine in skillet. Cook several minutes or until sauce has a medium-thick consistency. Return shrimp to skillet and toss to coat. Serve over slices of broiled Italian bread.

Panzanella

A bread salad, characteristic of Florence, is used as an antipasto. Use a good whole wheat bread several days old. This is a dish full of summer flavors.

1 lb. whole wheat bread, several days old
1 large red onion, sliced
10 fresh basil leaves, torn into pieces
2 large tomatoes, diced
salt and freshly ground pepper
1/3 cup olive oil
1 tbs. red wine vinegar

Soak bread in very cold water for 15 minutes. Squeeze to remove all liquid and place in a bowl. Place onion over bread, and then basil and tomatoes. Cover and refrigerate for 2 hours. Remove from refrigerator, season with salt and pepper and toss well with oil and vinegar. Serve on romaine lettuce leaves.

Carpaccio

Carpaccio is said to be created by Harry Cipriani, owner of Harry's Bar in Venice. It is thinly sliced raw sirloin served with a seasoned sauce.

1 lb. sirloin
½ lb. coarsely grated Parmesan cheese
1 tsp. Dijon mustard
juice of 2 lemons
salt and freshly ground pepper to taste
½ cup olive oil
3 tbs. capers

Slice meat into very, very thin slices. (Partially frozen meat will be easier to slice.) Place slices on individual plates. In a medium bowl, combine cheese, mustard, lemon juice, salt and pepper. Mix well. Whisk in olive oil and stir in the capers. Spoon over meat. Serve at room temperature.

Tortellini with Parsley-Caper Sauce

Servings: 6-8

This appetizer has a special festive presentation if you use red tortellini (with tomato pasta).

1 lb. meat or cheese tortellini
3 cloves garlic
½ cup grated Parmesan cheese
¼ cup sunflower seeds
¼ cup capers
1½ cups minced parsley
1 cup olive oil
salt and freshly ground pepper

Cook tortellini in boiling water just until done. Drain and toss with sauce or a bit of olive oil if not using at once. For sauce, drop garlic cloves into a food processor. Process until chopped. Add cheese, sunflower seeds, capers and parsley. Whir to a coarse puree. With the processor running, slowly pour in olive oil. Season to taste with salt and pepper. Place cooked tortellini in a warm, shallow bowl. Pour sauce over and toss. Serve with toothpicks.

Soups

Soup may not be the first thing that comes to mind when you think of Italian food, but there is an outstanding selection. The first course in an Italian meal is often a steaming bowl of soup. And the more hearty versions can be the entire meal.

Italy has a delightful repertoire of soups depending on the region. Each Coastal area will showcase its seafood in a soup. Northern Italy will add rice, the Italian Riviera, vegetables, the South, pasta and Tuscany will add beans.

In the North around Genoa, the soup may be predominantly green with the flavor of pesto. In the South near Naples and Salerno, the soup will be a base of tomatoes, onions and garlic. Bologna is known for its tortellini in a rich broth.

Whatever soup you choose, it will set the stage for and blend with the remainder of the meal.

SOUPS

Fresh Herb and Egg Soup

This quick and easy soup has the refreshing flavors of freshly chopped mint, basil and parsley. Beaten eggs are slowly added to the boiling broth to give it a thick consistency.

3 (14½ ozs. each) cans chicken broth
2 tbs. mint, chopped
3 tbs. fresh basil, chopped
2 tbs. parsley, chopped
2 whole eggs + 1 egg yolk
salt and freshly ground pepper to taste
freshly grated Parmesan cheese

Place chicken broth in a large saucepan and bring to a boil. Add herbs and cook for 2 minutes. Beat eggs and yolk in a small bowl with salt and pepper. Slowly pour this mixture into boiling broth, mixing with a whisk. Remove from heat and ladle into bowls. Serve with Parmesan cheese.

Minestrone

The name minestrone is derived from minestra, meaning "big soup." This minestrone is prepared with vegetables cooked in a bean-stock base. Minestrone varies from region to region, from household to household and from season to season.

1 lb. dried white beans
2 (14½ ozs. each) cans chicken or
   beef broth
8 cups water
½ lb. salt pork, cut into thick slices
½ cup olive oil
1 cup chopped onion
1 (8 ozs.) can tomato sauce
1 (28½ ozs.) can Italian plum
   tomatoes, broken up
1 cup chopped celery

1 cup chopped carrots
2 cups peeled, diced potatoes
1 cup of any or all of the following:
   chopped leeks
   diced zucchini
   green beans, sliced in small pieces
   wax beans, sliced in small pieces
   peas
   coarsely chopped cabbage
salt and freshly ground pepper to taste
grated Parmesan cheese

In large stockpot combine dried beans with broth and water. Bring to a boil. Boil for 2 minutes and then remove from heat. Let stand, covered, for 1 hour. Return to stove and add salt pork. Bring to a boil, cover and simmer for 2 hours or until beans are tender. Drain and save stock; discard salt pork. Reserve half the beans and puree remaining in a blender. In same stockpot heat olive oil over medium-high heat. Add chopped onion and cook until soft and golden. Add bean puree and cook for 2-3 minutes. Add reserved stock, reserved beans, tomato sauce, tomatoes, and vegetables. Bring to a boil, reduce heat, cover and simmer for 1½-2½ hours. Taste and add salt and pepper. Serve with grated Parmesan cheese.

Minestrone Genovese

Genoa is the home of this lovely green minestrone, which uses a meat stock instead of a bean base, to which fresh green vegetables are added. Spoonfuls of freshly made pesto are added to each serving.

2 (14½ ozs. each) cans chicken or
   beef broth
8 cups water
2 cups diced potato
2 cups sliced celery
1 onion, chopped
4 zucchini, diced

1 lb. green beans, cut in 2" lengths
½ cup elbow macaroni
1 cup peas
4 cups shredded cabbage
salt to taste
pesto

In a large stockpot combine chicken or beef broth and water. Bring to a boil. Add potatoes, reduce heat, cover and simmer for 10-15 minutes. Add celery, onion, zucchini, beans and macaroni and simmer uncovered for 5 minutes. Stir in peas and cabbage and cook an additional 6-8 minutes. Add salt to taste. Ladle soup into bowls and pass around pesto.

Escarole and Rice Soup

Escarole is a salad green that is also called broad-leaf endive. Use the tender inside leaves. These leaves are sautéed quickly in butter and onions and then simmered with rice in a chicken broth base.

1 head escarole
3 tbs. butter
2 tbs. finely chopped onion
2 (14½ ozs. each) cans chicken broth

½ cup rice (preferably Arborio rice)
salt and freshly ground pepper to taste
freshly grated Parmesan cheese

Remove coarse outer leaves of escarole. Wash and drain tender green leaves. Stack leaves and cut into ¼" wide strips. In large saucepan melt butter over medium-high heat. Add onion and sauté until browned. Add escarole strips and sauté for about 3 minutes. Add 1 can chicken broth and cook over low heat, covered, until escarole is tender, about 25 minutes. Add remaining broth, bring to a boil and add rice. Cover and cook until rice is done, about 15-20 minutes, stirring occasionally. Taste and adjust seasonings. Ladle into soup bowls and serve with Parmesan cheese.

Spinach Dumplings in Broth

Plump spinach dumplings float in a chicken broth for this tasty first course.

Dumplings
bread crumbs from 4-day-old white bread slices
2 tbs. grated Parmesan cheese
1 garlic clove, minced
⅓ cup frozen spinach, thawed and squeezed dry (about ¼ of 10 ozs. pkg.)
2 tbs. ricotta cheese
1 egg
⅛ tsp. salt
freshly ground pepper to taste

Broth
2 tbs. butter
2 celery stalks, minced
2 carrots, minced
1 onion, minced
3 (14½ ozs. each) cans chicken broth
4 cups water

Dumplings: Mix all dumpling ingredients in a medium bowl until well blended. With floured hands, shape mixture into 2" x ½" logs. Bring a large pot of salted water to a boil. Add dumplings. Adjust heat so liquid barely simmers. Dumplings are done when they just rise to surface, about 2 minutes. Remove with slotted spoon. Cut each dumpling into 5 or 6 slices.

Broth: In large saucepan melt butter over medium-high heat. Add celery, carrots and onion and sauté until tender but not brown, about 10 minutes. Stir in chicken broth and water, bring to a boil and simmer for 20 minutes. Add dumpling slices and simmer until heated through. Ladle into bowls.

Mushroom Soup

Fresh mushrooms star in this quick and easy soup. They are sautéed in olive oil and butter with onion and then combined with a beef broth and vermouth. It is an elegant beginning to an Italian meal.

3 tbs. olive oil
3 tbs. butter
1 large onion, finely chopped
1 lb. mushrooms, thinly sliced
3 tbs. tomato paste

5 cups beef broth
½ cup sweet vermouth
salt and freshly ground pepper to taste
freshly grated Parmesan cheese

Place olive oil and butter in a large saucepan over medium-high heat. Add onion and mushrooms and cook until onion is soft and translucent, stirring occasionally, about 10 minutes. Stir in tomato paste. Add broth and vermouth. Bring to a boil and simmer 10 minutes. Season with salt and pepper. Ladle into bowls and serve with Parmesan cheese.

Seafood Stew

The bounties of the Mediterranean are showcased in this tasty soup. Scallops, prawns and mussels are excellent for this dish as they do not fall apart when cooked.

4 tbs. olive oil
1 onion, finely chopped
1 clove garlic, minced
1 carrot, finely chopped
1 stalk celery, finely chopped
½ cup dry white wine

8 small- to-medium raw shrimp
20 mussels
½ lb. scallops, cut into small pieces
6 cups water
4 slices toast

Place olive oil in a large saucepan over medium-high heat. Add onion, garlic, carrot and celery and sauté until soft, and the onion is golden in color. Add wine, bring to a boil and let cook 1 minute. Add fish and water. Bring to a boil, reduce heat and let simmer for 20 minutes. Shell shrimp and mussels and return to soup. Place a slice of toast in the bottom of each soup bowl. Ladle soup into bowls and serve.

Clam Chowder

Use canned littleneck or whole baby clams, not minced clams.

1 stick butter
1 onion, chopped
¼ lb. pancetta, chopped
2 celery stalks, chopped
2 large carrots, chopped
3 large potatoes, diced

2 (8 ozs. each) bottles clam juice
12 large clams, chopped
  (or use oysters)
4 cups cream or half and half
salt and freshly ground pepper to taste

Over medium-high heat, melt ½ stick butter in a large saucepan. Add onion and pancetta and cook until onion is transparent. Add celery, carrots, potatoes and clam juice. Reduce heat to low and cook for about 20 minutes or until the potatoes are tender. Add clams (or oysters) and cream. DO NOT BOIL. Heat thoroughly. Add the remaining ½ stick butter and stir until it melts. Serve immediately.

Tortellini Soup

Servings: 6

Chase away the winter cold with this hearty soup. Italian sausage in a tomato base stock with tortellinis make a complete meal. All that is needed is a crusty loaf of bread and a glass of Chianti.

1 lb. Italian sausage, mild or spicy, casings removed
3 zucchini, sliced
1 green pepper, diced
1 onion, chopped
1 clove garlic, minced
½ tsp. oregano leaves, crushed

2 (14½ ozs. each) cans chicken broth
1 (28½ ozs.) can Italian plum tomatoes, cut in pieces
1 (6 ozs.) can tomato paste
1 (8 ozs.) can tomato sauce
1-1½ lbs. frozen or fresh tortellini
freshly grated Parmesan cheese

In large saucepan over medium-high heat, cook sausage, zucchini, green pepper, onion, garlic and oregano until sausage is cooked. Stir to separate meat. Add remaining ingredients and bring to a boil. Reduce heat, cover and simmer 10-15 minutes. Stir occasionally. Serve with Parmesan cheese.

Tuscan Bean Soup

A hearty, peasant soup from the Tuscany region.

1 lb. dried white beans
2 (14½ ozs. each) cans beef broth
6 cups water
6 tbs. olive oil
2 slices pancetta, chopped
2 carrots, chopped
2 celery stalks, chopped
1 medium onion, chopped

1 tsp. rosemary
2 tbs. chopped parsley
2 garlic cloves, chopped
1 tbs. flour
¼ cup tomato paste
salt and freshly ground pepper to taste
¼ lb. small shell pasta
½ cup grated Parmesan cheese

Place beans in a bowl, cover with water and soak overnight. Drain. Place beans in a Dutch oven along with beef broth, water, 2 tbs. olive oil, pancetta, carrots, celery and onion. Bring to a boil, reduce heat and simmer about 1-1½ hours. In a small saucepan, heat remaining 4 tbs. olive oil over medium heat. Add rosemary, parsley and garlic. Sauté about 5 minutes. Stir in flour and cook 1 minute. Stir in 1 cup liquid from the bean mixture and the tomato paste. Season with salt and pepper. Cook about 10 minutes. Add to the bean mixture.

With a slotted spoon, place about one-third of the beans into a blender. Puree until smooth. Return to pan. Bring soup to a boil and add the pasta. Cook about 8 minutes. Adjust seasonings. Stir in the Parmesan cheese. When serving, pass more Parmesan cheese around if desired.

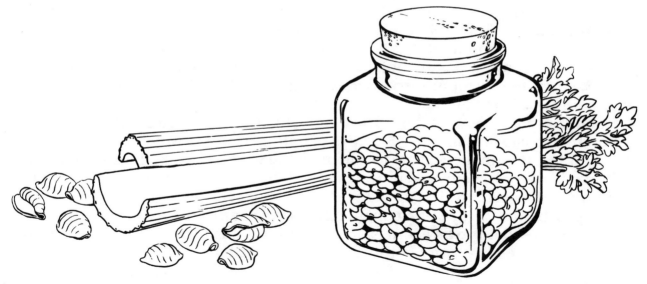

Pasta and Pasta Sauces

Pasta — an Italian treasure and the best known feature of Italian cooking —comes in a seemingly endless array of shapes and sizes. And to go with the pasta is a wide variety of sauces from fresh vegetables to meats and seafood.

Pasta from Southern Italy is usually solid (like spaghetti) or hollow (ziti) and is made without eggs. The sauces tend to be very robust and full flavored. Northern Italian pasta is often ribbon-shaped (fettucine) and is made with eggs. The sauces are slightly more delicate and often have a cream base.

When buying dried pasta, look for a top quality Italian pasta that is labeled ``100% semolina'' (ground durum wheat) and is a pale gold color. When cooked, it should double in volume.

Never overcook pasta. It should be tender, but firm to the bite (``al dente''). For 1 pound of pasta, use about 4-5 quarts of boiling water to which a little salt has been added. It is not necessary to add oil to the water. If cooked in this manner, the pasta will cook evenly and not stick together. There is no need to rinse pasta.

Enjoy all the wonderful pasta dishes in this chapter. When selecting the pasta to go with the sauce, take into consideration the shape and texture of the pasta. A light sauce should go on a thin pasta such as linguine or angel hair, and a more robust sauce needs a more hearty pasta such as ziti.

PASTA AND PASTA SAUCES

Pesto Sauce

Servings: 6 (as a first course)

There are several recipes for Genovese pesto which is a simple blend of fresh basil, pine nuts, Parmesan cheese, olive oil and garlic. This is a basic variation which is made in a blender. It keeps well in the freezer for several months.

2 cups fresh basil
½ cup olive oil
¼ cup pine nuts
2 cloves garlic
1 tsp. salt

freshly ground pepper to taste
½ cup grated Parmesan cheese
2 tbs. Romano cheese
3 tbs. butter at room temperature
1½ lbs. pasta

Place basil, oil, pine nuts, garlic, salt and pepper in a blender. Puree until evenly mixed. Using a rubber spatula, scrape into a bowl. Blend into the cheeses, and then beat in the butter. Before serving, add 1-2 tbs. hot water to pesto. Spoon over cooked pasta. Toss to coat pasta and serve.

Sun-Dried Tomatoes, Peppers and Basil Sauce

Servings: 6 (as a first course)

If you've never tasted sun-dried tomatoes, now is the time! Use a thin pasta such as angel hair or linguine.

3 tbs. butter
2 tbs. olive oil
10 sun-dried tomatoes, cured in oil, chopped
¼ cup chopped fresh basil
¼ cup chopped fresh parsley
4 garlic cloves, minced

2 red bell peppers, roasted, peeled and cut into strips
2 green bell peppers, roasted, peeled and cut into strips
salt and freshly ground pepper to taste
¼ cup grated Parmesan cheese
1 lb. pasta

Heat the butter and oil in a skillet over medium heat. Add tomatoes, basil, parsley, garlic and peppers. Sauté about 10 minutes. Season with salt and pepper.

Serve over warm pasta and sprinkle with cheese.

Basic Marinara Sauce

Servings: 6 (as a first course)

This basic tomato sauce is delicious over pasta. It is used in other dishes throughout the book.

¼ cup olive oil
4 garlic cloves, minced
1 (28 ozs.) can Italian plum tomatoes
12-15 fresh basil leaves (or 2 tsp. dry)
1 tsp. salt
1 tsp. pepper
2 tbs. Romano cheese (optional)
1 lb. pasta

Heat oil in a large skillet over medium heat. Add garlic and cook until garlic is lightly brown. Crush the tomatoes by hand or in a blender. Add to the pan along with basil, salt and pepper. Cook over high heat for 15 minutes, uncovered. Add Romano cheese if you wish. Serve over pasta.

Fresh Tomato Sauce

This is a marvelously fresh, uncooked tomato sauce. Make certain your tomatoes are very ripe.

¼ cup olive oil
2 tbs. minced garlic
3 lbs. very ripe tomatoes
½ cup coarsely chopped fresh basil
3 tbs. red wine vinegar
salt and freshly ground pepper to taste
1 lb. pasta

Heat 1 tbs. olive oil in a small skillet over medium heat. Add garlic and sauté for 2-3 minutes; do not brown. Transfer to a large nonmetal bowl. Coarsely chop tomatoes and add to the bowl along with the remaining oil, basil, vinegar, salt and pepper. Let stand for 6 hours. Serve over pasta.

Minted Tomato Sauce

Servings: 6 (as a first course)

A can of sun-ripened, hand picked San Marzano tomatoes together with mint, basil and toasted walnuts make a refreshing sauce for pasta.

½ cup chopped walnuts
⅓ cup olive oil
1 onion, finely chopped
2 garlic cloves, minced
1 (28 ozs.) can San Marzano tomatoes, or other Italian plum tomatoes
¼ cup dry white wine
¼ cup chopped fresh basil
¼ cup chopped fresh mint
salt and freshly ground pepper to taste
1 lb. pasta

Spread walnuts in a shallow pan and toast in a 350° oven for 10 minutes or until browned. Heat oil in a large skillet over medium heat. Sauté onion for 5 minutes or until soft. Add garlic, tomatoes, white wine, basil, mint, salt and pepper. Simmer for about 10 minutes. Serve over pasta.

Veal and Porcini Mushroom Sauce

Delicate veal and wild dried Italian mushrooms with their wonderful intense flavor make a superb combination. They are blended together with tomatoes.

1 oz. dried porcini mushrooms
1 cup white wine
1 stick butter
1 onion, sliced
1 lb. veal scaloppine, cut into ¼" strips
1 tsp. oregano
4 tomatoes, peeled, seeded and diced
1 lb. pasta

Place mushrooms in a small bowl. Add wine and let soak 30 minutes. Melt butter in a large saucepan over medium heat. Sauté onion and veal 5 minutes. Add oregano, cover and simmer for 20 minutes. Add mushrooms (with the wine) and tomatoes to the veal. Cover and simmer another 45 minutes. Serve over pasta.

Bucatini with Broccoli

Servings: 6 (as a first course)

Bucatini is a thin spaghetti with a hole through the middle. This is a peasant dish, economical to make and absolutely delicious.

2 lbs. fresh broccoli
5 tbs. olive oil
1 red hot chile pepper, minced
6 anchovy fillets, chopped
4 garlic cloves, minced
½ cup parsley, chopped
salt and freshly ground pepper to taste
1 lb. Bucatini

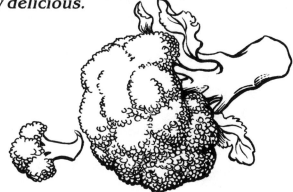

Separate the broccoli into florets. Peel the stalks and slice them. Steam the broccoli until tender but still crisp. Heat oil in a large skillet over medium heat. Add hot chile pepper, anchovies and garlic. Sauté 2 minutes. Stir in broccoli and parsley and season with salt and pepper. Cook another 5 minutes. Boil Bucatini in 4 quarts of salted water until tender but firm. Drain and place in a warm serving bowl. Add sauce and toss.

Rigatoni with Red Peppers

Servings: 6 (as a first course)

A touch of red wine vinegar adds a special zest to this fresh sauce of red bell peppers and tomatoes.

¼ cup olive oil
1 onion, chopped
3 red bell peppers, seeded and cut into strips
3 tomatoes, chopped
1 tsp. tomato paste
salt and freshly ground pepper to taste
2 tbs. red wine vinegar
1 lb. rigatoni

Heat oil in a large skillet over medium heat. Sauté onion and peppers until they have softened. Add tomatoes, paste, salt and pepper. Cover and simmer for 30 minutes. Add vinegar and cook another 10 minutes. Cook rigatoni in 4 quarts of boiling salted water until tender but firm. Drain and place in a warm serving bowl. Spoon the red pepper mixture over the top and serve.

Fusilli with Creamy Zucchini Sauce

Servings: 6
(as a first course)

This features fusilli, a spiral shaped pasta, together with a creamy cheese-based sauce with zucchini and basil.

3 tbs. olive oil
1 lb. zucchini, cut into strips
  or cubes
¼ lb. mushrooms, sliced
1 lb. fusilli
3 tbs. butter
3 tbs. olive oil

1 tsp. flour
⅓ cup milk
1 chicken bouillon cube
⅔ cup coarsely chopped fresh basil
1 egg yolk, lightly beaten
½ cup grated Parmesan cheese
¼ cup grated Pecorino Romano cheese

Heat 3 tbs. olive oil in a large skillet over medium heat. Add zucchini and mushrooms and sauté until the zucchini is lightly browned. Remove from skillet and set aside. Bring 4 quarts of water to boil. Add some salt and cook fusilli until tender but firm. While pasta is cooking, prepare the sauce. Place butter and olive oil in the skillet over medium heat. When butter foams, add flour and cook for 1 minute. Then slowly stir in milk. Add bouillon cube, basil and vegetables. Cook until heated through. Remove from heat and quickly beat in egg yolk and cheese. Drain cooked pasta. Place in a large serving bowl. Add sauce and toss thoroughly. Serve immediately.

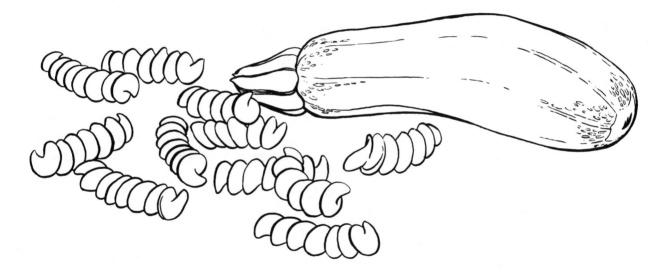

Penne Florentine

Penne is a hollow quill-shaped pasta. Here it is served with bacon, tomatoes and the ingredient that makes this "florentine," spinach.

6 slices bacon, diced
1 tbs. olive oil
4 garlic cloves, minced
2 tomatoes, seeded and chopped
⅔ cup grated Parmesan cheese
⅔ cup ricotta cheese

⅓ cup black olives, pitted and halved
salt and freshly ground pepper to taste
1 lb. penne
1½ lbs. fresh spinach,
    trimmed and chopped

In large skillet over medium heat, cook bacon until crisp. Remove from skillet and place in large bowl. Add olive oil and garlic to drippings in skillet. Sauté about 2 minutes. Add to bacon along with tomatoes, cheeses and olives. Season with salt and pepper. Cook penne in 4 quarts of boiling salted water. Place spinach in colander. Drain pasta over spinach to wilt spinach leaves. Add both pasta and spinach to bacon-tomato mixture. Toss well to combine and serve.

Fettucine with Peas and Mushrooms

This is a peasant pasta dish of prosciutto, peas and mushrooms blended together with cheese and cream.

1 stick butter
3 tbs. olive oil
¾ lb. mushrooms, sliced
1 beef bouillon cube
½ onion, diced
3 garlic cloves, minced

1 cup grated Romano cheese
1 tsp. pepper
2 cups heavy cream
½ lb. prosciutto
1 (10 ozs.) pkg. frozen peas, thawed
1 lb. fettucine

Place half the stick of butter and olive oil in a large skillet over medium heat. When butter has melted, add mushrooms, bouillon cube, onion and garlic. Sauté about 10 minutes. Remove from heat. In another skillet, melt the remaining half stick of butter. Add cheese, stirring with a whisk. Add pepper and cream, stirring constantly. Cook until sauce has thickened, about 10 minutes. Add prosciutto, peas and sautéed mushroom mixture and mix well. Cook about 5 minutes. Cook fettucine in 4 quarts of boiling salted water. Drain and place in serving bowl. Toss with the sauce and serve.

Spaghetti alla Carbonara

Servings: 6 (as a first course)

This means "charcoal burner's style" and is a favorite in Rome. Every trattoria claims its own "secret" variation. The egg yolks cook as they are mixed into the warm spaghetti.

1 tbs. olive oil
¼ lb. bacon, diced
4 egg yolks
¼ cup heavy cream
½ cup grated Parmesan cheese
½ cup chopped parsley
salt and freshly ground pepper to taste
1 lb. spaghetti

Place oil in a large skillet and warm over medium heat. Fry bacon until crisp. Remove skillet from heat and set aside. In a medium bowl, beat egg yolks. Add cream, cheese and parsley. Season with salt and pepper. Cook spaghetti in 4 quarts of boiling salted water. Drain and place in serving bowl. Stir in bacon and oil. Add the egg mixture and toss to coat pasta. Serve immediately.

Scallops with Spinach Fettucine
Servings: 4 (as a first course)

A blend of tender-crisp vegetables, scallops and cream dress the spinach fettucine. If you use large scallops, it may be necessary to slice them.

1 stick butter
2 large carrots, slivered
1 red bell pepper, seeded and
   slivered
8 scallions, slivered

⅔ cup dry white wine
1 lb. bay scallops
1½ cups heavy cream
½ lb. spinach fettucine
salt and freshly ground pepper to taste

Heat half the stick of butter in a large skillet over medium heat. Add carrots, bell pepper and scallions. Cook until slightly limp but still crisp. Remove from skillet. To the same pan, add wine and bring to a boil. Add scallops and cook just until the scallops are opaque, about 3 minutes. Remove scallops from pan and set aside. Add cream to the pan and bring to a boil. Reduce the liquid until it measures about 1½ cups. Turn the heat to low and stir in the remaining half stick butter until it melts. Meanwhile, cook fettucine until just tender. Drain and add to cream. Coat the pasta by lifting with two forks. Add scallops and vegetables and mix gently. Season to taste with salt and pepper.

Linguine with White Clam Sauce

Servings: 6 (as a first course)

A very light sauce with the sweet taste of clams is the perfect topping for linguine.

¼ cup olive oil
1 stick butter
2 cloves garlic, minced
2 cups whole canned clams
1½ cups clam juice (from clams)
½ cup chopped parsley
¼ tsp. pepper
1 lb. linguine

In a large skillet over medium heat, warm olive oil and melt butter. Add garlic cloves and sauté 2 minutes. Add clams. Simmer 10 minutes. Add clam juice (if you do not have 1½ cups liquid, add water or white wine to make it up). Add parsley and pepper. Taste for salt and add if needed. Simmer the sauce until it has cooked down to a thick consistency, about 15 minutes. Cook linguine until just tender. Drain, top with sauce and serve.

Vermicelli with Crab

Servings: 6 (as a first course)

A very thin pasta served with a light crab sauce. Add sliced artichoke hearts if you like.

4 tbs. butter
1 onion, chopped
3 garlic cloves, minced
3 celery stalks, chopped
1 red bell pepper, diced
¼ cup chopped parsley

2 tbs. lemon juice
2 tsp. chopped fresh basil
1 lb. crab, cooked and shredded
¾ cup chopped walnuts
salt and freshly ground pepper to taste
1 lb. vermicelli

Melt butter in a large skillet over medium heat. Add onion and sauté until soft, about 5 minutes. Add garlic, celery, and bell pepper. Cook another 5 minutes. Add parsley, lemon juice, basil and crab. Cook about 5 minutes. Stir in walnuts. Season with salt and pepper. Cook pasta in 4 quarts of boiling water until firm but tender. Drain and place in a serving bowl. Toss with the sauce and serve.

Tuna Conchiglie

Servings: 6 (as a first course)

This is "conchiglie" or small shell-shaped pasta with a tuna fish sauce, which has the best flavor if you only heat the tuna and don't cook it.

5 tbs. olive oil
3 garlic cloves, minced
2 red bell peppers, roasted,
   skinned and cut into strips
¼ cup chopped parsley

2 tbs. capers
2 tbs. lemon juice
salt and freshly ground pepper to taste
1 (6½ ozs.) can tuna, packed in oil
1 lb. shell pasta

Warm the oil in a large skillet over medium heat. Sauté garlic for 2 minutes. Add peppers and cook for 5 minutes. Add parsley, capers, lemon juice, salt and pepper. Cook for 1-2 minutes. Add tuna, with oil, shredding it with a fork. Mix thoroughly and remove from heat. Cook pasta in 4 quarts of boiling salted water. When tender but firm, drain and transfer to a serving bowl. Toss with the sauce and serve.

Farfalle with Chicken Livers

This is bowtie-shaped pasta with a marvelous sauce, which is also good with wide noodles such as pappardelle and tagliatelle.

4 tbs. butter
2 tbs. olive oil
1 cup thinly sliced onion
½ lb. mushrooms, sliced
¼ cup pancetta, diced
1 lb. chicken livers, quartered

½ cup white wine
1 tbs. tomato paste
salt and freshly ground pepper to taste
½ tsp. sage
2 tbs. minced parsley
1 lb. farfalle

Heat butter and oil in a large skillet over medium heat. Sauté onion about 5 minutes. Add mushrooms and pancetta and cook another 5 minutes. Add chicken livers, stir and cook until they have lost their raw red color. Add wine, tomato paste, salt, pepper, sage and parsley. Stir well and cook for about 10 minutes or until liquid is reduced. When sauce is nearly done, cook pasta in 4 quarts of boiling salted water. Drain and transfer to a warm platter. Add the sauce, toss and serve.

Tagliatelle Bolognese

Servings: 4 (as a first course)

Among the myriad of Bolognese culinary claims is that they hold the secret to the finest meat sauce. This is an excellent sampling of their sauce.

2 tbs. olive oil
1 onion, chopped
2 celery stalks, diced
2 carrots, diced
3 garlic cloves, minced
¼ lb. pancetta, chopped
¼ lb. ground veal
½ lb. ground pork

¼ lb. ground beef
¼ cup chopped parsley
2 tbs. chopped fresh basil
1 (14½ ozs.) can tomatoes
1 (6 ozs.) can tomato paste
1 cup beef broth
1 cup red wine

Heat olive oil in a large pot over medium heat. Add onion, celery, carrots, garlic and pancetta. Cook for 3-4 minutes. Add meats and cook for 10 minutes. Add parsley, basil, tomatoes, tomato paste, broth and red wine. Simmer for about 45 minutes. Serve over pasta. Sprinkle with Parmesan or Romano cheese.

Other First Courses

The Italians have many culinary delights to be served as first courses other than a bowl of soup or plate of pasta.

In some northern sections of Italy, rice is served as often or more often than pasta. Risotto is the most common rice dish. It is always served as a first course rather than an accompaniment to the second course of meat, poultry or fish. There are many variations of risotto with herbs, vegetables, cheese, sausage and shellfish. This chapter gives you several different ways to prepare risotto.

Almost every region of Italy has its own version of gnocchi. Whether potato, flour or spinach, they are like a dumpling and served with a sauce.

Polenta is a cornmeal mush that can be served when just made or cooled, sliced and then grilled or fried. It is a staple of Northern Italy. In Venice it accompanies most main dishes or can be served as an appetizer, cut into small pieces, topped with cheese and broiled. However it is served, it is not eaten alone. Originally polenta was made in a ''paiolo'' (a large copper pot) which was suspended in the fireplace directly over the fire.

We also include other delicious dishes to make as the first course in your Italian meal, such as crab-stuffed shells, eggplant rollettes and crespelles.

OTHER FIRST COURSES

Rice Pilaf

Cappelli d'angelo is Italian for "angel's hair," a very thin, delicate pasta.

1 stick butter
½ onion, chopped
2 handfuls angel hair pasta
1 cup arborio rice
2½ cups chicken broth
freshly ground pepper to taste

Melt butter in a large saucepan over medium high heat. Add onion and pasta and brown well. Wash rice and stir into onion and pasta. Mix well. Add chicken broth and black pepper. Cover and cook over low heat for 25 minutes. Serve immediately.

Basic Risotto

Although risotto has been compared to pasta courses, there is at least one difference. Pasta is cooked first and then tossed with a sauce. Risotto cooks along with its condiments. The Italian rice "arborio" has a starch with special binding qualities to achieve the clinging but firm consistency that is characteristic of risotto. Risotto can be made with many ingredients such as vegetables, cheese, shellfish, or sausage. Whatever the ingredients, the cooking technique is the same. The rice is first briefly sautéed with butter and oil plus onion or garlic. Then small quantities of broth or water are added slowly while the rice is stirred. It swells, absorbs flavor and becomes creamy.

For this pure risotto, we add only Parmesan cheese.

7-8 cups chicken broth
¼ cup butter
1 onion, finely chopped
2½ cups arborio rice
¾ cup freshly grated Parmesan cheese
1 tbs. butter
salt

Bring broth to a simmer in a saucepan. In another large saucepan over medium heat, melt butter. Add onion and sauté about 5 minutes. Add rice and sauté 1-2 minutes. Add ½ cup of hot broth, stirring constantly. When rice has absorbed broth, add another ½ cup and continue to stir. Continue to add liquid as rice dries out. The risotto is done when the rice is tender but firm to the bite. It should take about 20-25 minutes. Add the cheese and 1 tbs. butter about 5 minutes before rice is done. Season with salt and serve.

Seafood Risotto

Scallops or shrimp can be used. Or, you can either substitute or add clams. As is true of this or any pasta or soup with a seafood base, this should not be made with grated cheese.

1½ lbs. scallops, or small shrimp, shelled and deveined
1 onion, chopped
3 tbs. butter
3 tbs. olive oil

3 garlic cloves, minced
¼ cup chopped parsley
2½ cups arborio rice
½ cup dry white wine
salt and freshly ground pepper to taste

Chop the scallops or shrimp into small pieces. Bring 5 cups of water to a simmer. In a large saucepan over medium heat, sauté onion in butter and olive oil about 5 minutes. Add garlic and parsley. Stir in rice and add wine. When the wine is absorbed add water ½ cup by ½ cup, until rice is tender but firm to the bite (see basic recipe). When rice is 5 minutes from being done, add seafood. Season with salt and pepper.

Potato Gnocchi

Gnocchi is the name for Italian dumplings. The Piedmont region is considered the capital of gnocchi. This is a basic gnocchi using potatoes. They can be eaten with butter and Parmesan or with almost any sauce: red, white, pesto, mushroom, etc.

8 medium potatoes (russets)
1 egg yolk
1 tbs. salt

2½ cups flour
¼ cup butter
⅔ cup grated Parmesan cheese

Boil potatoes until tender. Drain and peel. In a large bowl mash potatoes with a mixer or through a ricer or food mill. Add egg yolk, salt and flour. Turn out on floured work surface and knead into a ball. With floured hands, shape dough into rolls 1" long. Place each roll on inside of fork and press against tines with tip of finger. Boil the gnocchi (20 at a time) in 5 quarts of boiling water. When they float to surface, cook 15 seconds. Drain and serve with butter and cheese (or your favorite sauce).

Gnocchi Verde

These are spinach and ricotta gnocchi which can be served with Marinara sauce. The gnocchi can be boiled or baked.

¼ cup butter
2 (10 ozs. each) pkgs. frozen chopped spinach,
    thawed, squeezed dry and finely minced
1¼ cups ricotta cheese
1 cup grated Parmesan cheese
1 cup flour
4 eggs, beaten
¾ tsp. salt
freshly ground pepper to taste
Marinara sauce
    or
grated Parmesan cheese

Melt butter in a heavy skillet over medium heat. Add spinach and sauté a few minutes to evaporate moisture. Add ricotta and continue cooking for 10 minutes, stirring constantly. Turn into a large bowl. Add Parmesan, flour, eggs, salt and pepper. Blend well. Bring 4 quarts of salted water to a rapid boil. Dust hands with flour. Shape mixture into balls about 1" in diameter. Add gnocchi to the water, reduce heat to simmer gently, and cook about 3 minutes. Remove with slotted spoon. **Or**, place uncooked gnocchi in a buttered baking dish. Drizzle with ¼ cup melted butter and bake in 425° oven for 12-14 minutes. Serve gnocchi with Marinara sauce **or** sprinkled with melted butter and grated Parmesan cheese.

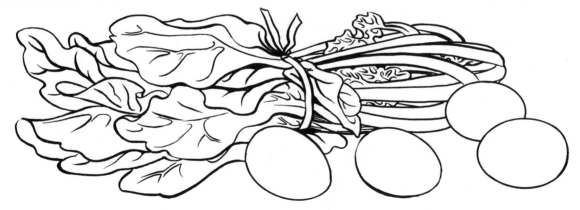

Baked Cannellini Beans

Servings: 6

This is a very Mediterranean version of white beans baked in a casserole with prosciutto, garlic, sage and tomatoes.

3 cups dried cannellini beans
¼ lb. prosciutto, diced
2 garlic cloves, minced
2 tbs. minced fresh sage
¼ cup olive oil
1 large tomato, peeled, seeded and diced
salt and freshly ground pepper

Soak beans, covered with water, in a bowl overnight. Drain, rinse and place in an oven-proof casserole. Add prosciutto, garlic, sage, olive oil and tomato to beans. Add enough water to cover beans. Sprinkle with salt and pepper. Cover casserole and bake in a 375° oven for 2½ hours. Stir every 30 minutes. Remove from oven, cool 10 minutes and serve.

Basic Polenta

A traditional dish and a staple in Northern Italy, polenta consists of cornmeal and water. It is important to stir the cornmeal and water constantly for a smooth consistency.

9 cups water   3 cups cornmeal
1½ tbs. salt

Bring water and salt to a boil in a large saucepan. Reduce heat and add cornmeal *very slowly*, stirring constantly with a long-handled wooden spoon. Continuing to stir, cook 20-30 minutes or until polenta is very thick and comes away cleanly from sides of pan. Spoon polenta onto a large platter. Using wet hands, smooth it out to a 2" thickness. As it cools (about 10 minutes), it will solidify. Cut into slices. Serve with butter and cheese or a sauce such as Bolognese or Marinara.

***Variations:* Fried Polenta** — Heat 1" of vegetable oil in a skillet and fry slices of polenta on both sides until golden.
Broiled Polenta — Place slices of polenta on broiler pan. Brush with melted butter or sprinkle with Gorgonzola cheese and broil until golden brown.

Polenta with Sausage

For a satisfying meal, start with roasted peppers and mozzarella (see appetizers) and omit the pasta or rice course. This, although a second course, also replaces the first course.

½ onion, chopped
¼ cup olive oil
¼ cup diced carrots
¼ cup diced celery
¼ lb. pancetta, diced

1 lb. sweet Italian sausage
1 cup canned Italian plum tomatoes
salt and freshly ground pepper to taste
Polenta (see basic Polenta recipe)

Sauté onion in olive oil about 5 minutes in a large skillet over medium heat. Add the carrots, celery and pancetta. Sauté another 5 minutes. Remove sausage from its casing and add to the pan. Cook for about 10 minutes or until sausage is brown. Add tomatoes and simmer 20 minutes. Season with salt and pepper. Keep warm. Cook polenta and pour onto a large platter. Make a well in the center and pour in the sausage mixture.

Spinach Crespelle

These are very thin pancakes with a ricotta-spinach filling. The crespelle can be made days ahead and refrigerated or frozen.

Filling
1½ lbs. ricotta
1 egg
2 tbs. grated Romano cheese
1 (10 ozs.) pkg. frozen chopped
    spinach, thawed and drained
salt and freshly ground pepper to taste

Crespelle
4 eggs
¾ cup milk
1 cup flour
dash salt

Marinara sauce (page 44)

Filling: In a large bowl mix ricotta, egg and Romano cheese together. Stir in spinach and blend well. Taste for salt and pepper. Set aside.

Crespelle: Place ingredients in blender and blend well.

Pour just enough batter in crepe pan or small frying pan to coat bottom of pan. Tip pan to smooth out the batter. Cook until just done. Flip and cook for a few seconds. Place crespelle between sheets of waxed paper to cool. Fill crespelles with spinach-ricotta mixture, roll and place into baking dish which has thin layer of Marinara sauce in it. Spoon remaining sauce over top. Bake in 350° oven for 20 minutes.

Eggplant Rollettes

These are slices of eggplant, floured, sautéed and then rolled around a tasty filling with ricotta cheese. They are topped with Marinara sauce and mozzarella cheese.

1 eggplant
1 cup flour
salt and pepper
3 eggs, beaten lightly
1 cup vegetable oil

Marinara sauce
½ lb. sliced mozzarella cheese

Filling
1 lb. ricotta
1 egg
¼ cup chopped parsley
2 tbs. Romano cheese
salt and freshly ground pepper to taste

Slice eggplant lengthwise into very thin slices. Dip slices into flour seasoned with salt and pepper. Then dip slices into beaten eggs. Heat oil in a large frying pan over medium heat. Sauté eggplant until golden brown. Drain on paper towels and set aside. In a large bowl mix all the filling ingredients together.

Spoon a heaping tablespoon onto each slice of eggplant and roll up. Spoon a layer of Marinara sauce on the bottom of a large baking dish. Place eggplant rolls in the dish in a single layer. Cover with remaining sauce and top with sliced mozzarella. Cover with foil and bake 30 minutes at 350°.

Pesto Potatoes

Servings: 8

Cooked, cubed potatoes are marvelous drizzled with virgin olive oil and topped with fresh pesto.

3 lbs. white potatoes, peeled
salt to taste
2 tbs. olive oil, good quality
1/2 cup pesto, page 40

Bring water, potatoes and salt to a boil in a large saucepan. Let potatoes boil until cooked but firm, about 20 to 30 minutes. Remove potatoes from water and while still hot, cut into 1-inch cubes. Place potato cubes in a serving dish and toss gently with olive oil. When cooled, top with pesto sauce and serve.

Meats

With little grazing land available in Italy, Italians are not great red meat eaters. Yet, they still produce top quality beef in the pastures of Tuscany. Steaks are either grilled or pan-broiled while larger cuts of meat are cooked slowly with wine, herbs and vegetables.

Veal is probably the most famous Italian meat dish. Veal is from an 8 to 10-week-old calf fed on a diet of dried milk and eggs. Very lean, it will become dry and tough if not handled properly in the cooking process. The choicest cut is scaloppine and should be cooked very briefly over high heat. Other veal dishes are most often braised.

Italians also eat quite a bit of pork, especially in the form of sausage, ham, pancetta and prosciutto. The array of sausages in a "salumerie" is endless.

Aside from fresh meats, the list of Italian smoked and cured meats is impressive. However, these meats are generally served as an antipasto and not a main-course meat. All the recipes in this chapter are for a main (or second) course meat dish.

MEATS

Veal in Lemon-Cream Sauce

Servings: 4

Veal and lemon are a classic pair. The cream smooths out the sauce.

1 lb. veal scaloppine
2 tbs. flour
2 tbs. olive oil
12 mushrooms, cut in half
1 clove garlic, minced

salt and freshly ground pepper to taste
2 tbs. butter
¼ cup white wine
juice of ½ lemon
½ cup heavy cream

Lightly dust veal with flour. Heat oil in a large skillet over high heat. Sauté veal and mushrooms until veal is lightly browned on both sides. Add garlic and sauté 1 minute. Season with salt and pepper. Transfer veal to a platter. Add butter to the skillet. When melted, add white wine and lemon juice. Add cream and cook over high heat until sauce begins to thicken. Return veal to skillet and heat. Serve immediately.

Suggested Menu Plan First Course: Gnocchi Verde, **or** Pasta with Sun-Dried
Tomatoes, Peppers and Basil Sauce
Vegetables: Asparagus with Parmesan Cheese, **or** Peas
with Pine Nuts

Veal Scaloppines in Basil Sauce

It is best not to make scaloppines for more than six people unless you are skillful at handling more than one skillet at a time. These are rolled around a flavorful filling and topped with a fresh basil sauce.

Filling
1 lb. ricotta cheese
¼ cup chopped fresh basil
2 tsp. minced fresh sage (¾ tsp. dry)
2 tsp. minced fresh oregano
   (¾ tsp. dry)
salt and freshly ground pepper
   to taste

Sauce
1 cup dry white wine
½ cup fresh basil leaves and stems
2 tbs. minced shallots
1½ sticks unsalted butter, sliced
¼ cup chopped fresh basil
salt and freshly ground pepper to taste

1½ lbs. veal scaloppine, pounded thin
1 cup flour
¼ stick butter
2 tbs. olive oil

In a medium bowl, combine all the filling ingredients. Place 2 tbs. filling in center of each veal scaloppine. Fold edges over and roll up. Cover and refrigerate up to 3 hours.

To prepare sauce: In a small saucepan, combine the wine, basil and shallots. Cook over medium-high heat until reduced to about ¼ cup. Strain into a heavy saucepan and discard herbs. Over very low heat, whisk in butter, one slice at a time. Stir in chopped basil. Season with salt and pepper. Keep warm.

Dip veal rolls in flour. In a large skillet melt butter and warm oil over high heat. Add veal rolls, seam side down, and cook until golden brown, turning, about 2-3 minutes per side. Serve immediately with basil sauce.

Suggested Menu Plan   First Course: Mushroom Soup **or** Escarole and Rice Soup, **or**
Fresh Tomato Sauce over pasta
Vegetable: Braised Celery **or** Spinach and Prosciutto

Veal Marsala

The best of the Italian veal dishes, it can be prepared in just a few minutes.

½ cup flour
salt and freshly ground pepper
1 lb. veal scaloppine
1 stick butter

2 tbs. olive oil
1 cup Marsala wine
1 beef bouillon cube
2 tbs. chopped parsley

On a plate combine flour, salt and pepper. Coat veal with seasoned flour. Melt butter and warm oil in a large skillet over high heat. Add veal and sauté very quickly. Remove veal to a warm platter. Add wine and bouillon cube to drippings in skillet, stirring to loosen browned bits. Add parsley and stir. Return veal to pan. Mix gently and heat through. Serve immediately.

Suggested Menu Plan First Course: Spinach Crespelle **or** Risotto
Vegetable: Broccoli **or** Braised Swiss Chard

Braised Veal Roast

This marvelous dish is from Venice. The cooking liquid can be strained and used as the base for a soup.

2 tbs. butter
2 tbs. olive oil
3 lbs. boneless veal loin roast
1 onion, chopped
2 carrots, sliced

2 celery stalks, sliced
1 cup chicken broth
juice of 2 lemons
salt and freshly ground pepper to taste

Heat butter and oil in a Dutch oven over medium-high heat. Add the veal roast and brown on all sides. Add vegetables and sauté 5 minutes. Pour in broth and lemon juice. Season with salt and pepper. Cover and simmer 1½-2 hours or until veal is tender. Remove veal and thinly slice. Serve. Strain stock and save to be used as a soup base if desired.

Suggested Menu Plan   First Course: Tagliatelle Bolognese **or** Rigatoni with Red Peppers
Vegetable: Baked Onions **or** Carrots with Gorgonzola

Sautéed Veal Chops

The veal chops are browned and then topped with a smooth sauce flavored with lemon juice, capers and dry vermouth.

2 tbs. butter
3 tbs. olive oil
6 veal chops, cut ½"-¾" thick
salt and freshly ground pepper to taste
½ cup beef broth

⅓ cup dry vermouth
2 tbs. lemon juice
⅔ cup heavy cream
2 tbs. capers, drained
3 tbs. minced parsley

Heat butter and oil in a large skillet over medium-high heat. Add veal chops and brown on both sides. Season with salt and pepper. Cook until pink in center. Transfer to platter and keep in warm oven. Add broth, vermouth and lemon juice to the skillet. Boil until reduced to half. Stir in cream, capers and parsley. Simmer until slightly thickened. Pour sauce over veal chops and serve.

Suggested Menu Plan   First Course: Gnocchi **or** Risotto
Vegetable: Zucchini and Tomatoes with Herbs

Filets fra Diavola

Although Italians know the virtues of broiling steaks, they also appreciate the delectable results of pan broiling.

2 tbs. butter
¼ cup olive oil
4 filet mignons, or other good quality steak
salt and freshly ground pepper to taste
½ cup Marsala wine

½ cup white wine
3 garlic cloves, minced
½ tsp. chopped hot red pepper
3 tbs. chopped parsley

In a skillet just large enough to hold the steaks, heat butter and oil over high heat. Add steaks and pan broil until brown on both sides. Season with salt and pepper. Remove meat to warm platter. Add wines to skillet and stir to loosen any meat residues. Add garlic and hot red pepper and cook for 1 minute. Return steaks to pan and coat them with sauce. Transfer to platter and cover with sauce. Sprinkle with parsley and serve.

Suggested Menu Plan   First Course: Escarole and Rice Soup, **or** Risotto **or** Spaghetti
alla Carbonara
Vegetable: Braised Swiss Chard **or** Broccoli

Braciole alla Palermo

This dish, found in all regions of Italy, is made from a thin slice of meat that is rolled up over a variety of fillings. This one is a Sicilian version. It is delicious and extremely simple to prepare.

1½ lbs. boned round steak, cut thin
olive oil
salt and freshly ground pepper
   to taste
¼ cup chopped parsley
2 cloves garlic, minced
¼ cup grated Romano cheese
2 tbs. chopped bell pepper

½ cup fresh bread crumbs
4 slices prosciutto
¼ cup olive oil
1 onion, chopped
1 cup dry white wine
1 (28 ozs.) can Italian plum tomatoes
2 tbs. chopped fresh oregano
salt and freshly ground pepper to taste

Pound steak between sheets of waxed paper until very thin. Brush with olive oil and sprinkle with salt and pepper. In a medium bowl, combine parsley, garlic, cheese, bell pepper and bread crumbs. Spread over steak. (Mixture at this point will be very dry, but will become moist in the cooking stage.) Lay slices of prosciutto on top. Fold in sides of steak and roll up tightly. Tie securely with string. Heat olive oil in a large sauté pan over high heat. Brown steak on all sides. Add onion and cook 10 minutes. Add wine and cook over high heat about 10 minutes. Stir in tomatoes, cover and cook over low heat for 1 hour. Add oregano; season with salt and pepper and cook another 10 minutes. Lift meat from the pan. Remove the strings and slice the meat. Arrange on a serving platter or individual plates and serve.

Suggested Menu Plan   First Course: Tuscan Bean Soup **or** Minestrone **or** Fusilli with Creamy Zucchini Sauce
Vegetable: Braised Fennel

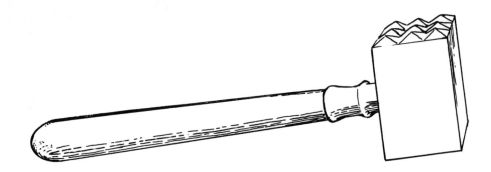

Braised Beef in Barolo

Barolo, a fine red wine from the Piedmont region, gives the maximum flavor to this beef dish.

2 tbs. butter
2 tbs. olive oil
3 lbs. beef rump or bottom round roast
1 onion, coarsely chopped
3 celery stalks, chopped
2 carrots, chopped
¼ lb. pancetta, diced
1 tsp. majoram
1 tsp. thyme
2 bay leaves
⅛ tsp. cinnamon
3 cups Barolo wine
salt and freshly ground pepper to taste

In a heavy casserole, just bigger than the beef, heat butter and oil over high heat. Brown meat on all sides and remove. Add onion, celery, carrots and pancetta. Sauté 5 minutes over medium-high heat. Add herbs and pour in wine. Stir well and simmer 10 minutes. Return meat to casserole. Season with salt and pepper. Cover and simmer gently for 1½-2 hours or until meat is tender. Turn beef occasionally. Add beef broth if necessary to keep beef almost covered with liquid. Remove meat from casserole. Strain liquid and boil about 10 minutes to reduce. Slice meat, spoon sauce over slices and serve.

Suggested Menu Plan   First Course: Spinach Dumplings in Broth **or** Gnocchi Verde
Vegetable: Baked Eggplant **or** Green Beans and Peppers with Tomatoes

Roast Leg of Lamb

Lamb is a seasonal dish in Italy, often served at Easter. Here the lamb is marinated with a mixture of garlic, rosemary and parsley.

1 leg of lamb (6-7 lbs.)
6-8 garlic cloves, minced
2 cups parsley, finely chopped
⅓ cup crumbled dry rosemary **or** ½ cup fresh rosemary, finely chopped
½ tbs. grated lemon peel
½ tsp. salt
1 tsp. freshly ground pepper
⅓ cup olive oil
3 tbs. butter, melted and cooled
dry white wine
rosemary and parsley sprigs for garnish

Trim lamb of all fat, gristle and skin. In a small bowl, mix together garlic, parsley, rosemary and lemon peel. With a sharp knife, make tiny pockets all over meat. Push some of the garlic/parsley mixture into each pocket. Combine olive oil and butter in a small bowl. Rub meat with salt and pepper and then with olive oil/butter mixture. Cover with plastic wrap and refrigerate overnight to let flavors permeate meat.

Place meat on a rack in a roasting pan. Insert meat thermometer if desired. Add 1 inch of white wine to pan. Cook in a 400° oven for 15 minutes. Reduce heat to 325° and cook until tender, about 3 hours or until internal thermometer registers 180°. Baste frequently with pan juices, adding more wine if needed, always keeping 1 inch liquid in pan.

Remove from oven, let rest 5 to 10 minutes, and carve. Garnish with rosemary and parsley sprigs and serve.

Suggested Menu Plan   First Course: Gnocchi Verde **or** Fettucini with Peas and
                    Mushrooms
                    Vegetable: Broccoli with Garlic and Lemon

---

Pork Roast Braised in Milk

A pork loin braised in milk is quite an Italian delicacy. The milk "disappears" and is replaced by a flavorful brown sauce.

3 tbs. butter
3 tbs. olive oil
3½ lbs. boneless pork loin roast
salt and freshly ground pepper to taste
2 garlic cloves, minced
1 bay leaf
3 cups milk

Heat butter and oil in a large casserole over medium-high heat. Add pork roast and brown on all sides. Season with salt and pepper. Add garlic and sauté for 1 minute. Add bay leaf and milk. Partially cover casserole and cook over low heat for 2½ hours. Baste pork several times during cooking. Add more milk if necessary. During final 10-15 minutes of cooking, uncover, raise heat and cook until milk darkens and only brown clusters remain. Remove meat and slice.

Arrange on a warm serving platter. Remove as much fat as possible from sauce. Add 3 tbs. water and stir to loosen particles from bottom of casserole. Spoon sauce over pork slices and serve.

Suggested Menu Plan   First Course: Tagliatelle Bolognese **or** Semolina Gnocchi
Vegetable: Asparagus with Parmesan cheese **or** Carrots with Gorgonzola

---

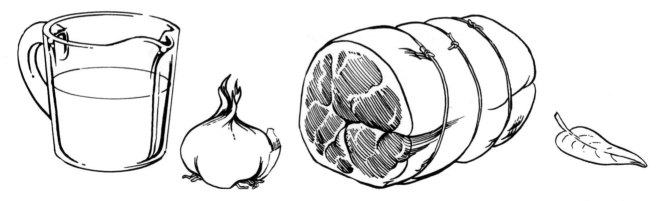

Roast Pork Tenderloin

The blending of olive oil, rosemary and pork make an outstanding dish.

3-4 lbs. pork tenderloin
2 tbs. olive oil
1 tbs. lemon juice
1 tbs. rosemary
salt and freshly ground pepper to taste

¼ stick butter
¼ cup minced onion
2 tbs. flour
1 cup dry white wine
¼ cup grated Parmesan cheese

Remove any excess fat from pork. Rub with olive oil and lemon juice. Sprinkle with rosemary, salt and pepper, pressing into meat. Place tenderloins on rack in a roasting pan. Roast, uncovered, in 325° oven for 2½-3 hours. Remove meat from pan and cover with foil to keep warm. Melt butter in a saucepan over medium-high heat. Add onion and sauté 5 minutes. Whisk in flour and cook for 1 minute. Stir in wine and simmer a few minutes until sauce is slightly thickened. Stir in cheese. Slice pork and serve with sauce.

Suggested Menu Plan First Course: Mushroom Soup **or** Fettucine with Peas and Mushrooms
Vegetable: Zucchini and Tomatoes with Herbs **or** Braised Celery

Poultry

Many of Italy's best known and finest dishes are based on chicken. It can be roasted whole or grilled on a spit. It can be cut into parts and pan roasted, broiled, baked or stewed and served with a variety of sauces.

Chicken can be prepared simply by marinating in olive oil and lemon juice and then quick pan-roasting. Or, Italians will combine vegetables and herbs in a hearty tomato sauce for a chicken cacciatore dish. Boned and skinned chicken breasts are flattened, spread with prosciutto and cheese, rolled and then baked.

Italians also make use of other poultry such as squab and quail. We have chosen to include only chicken because it is the most readily available.

There is a wide variety of flavors in these chicken dishes.

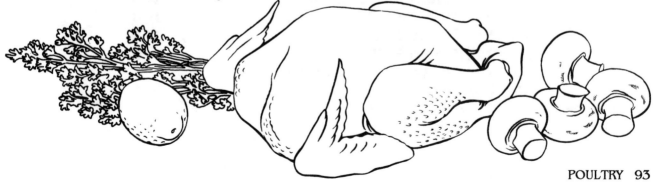

POULTRY

Chicken with Prosciuttini and Wine

Prosciuttini is an Italian ham, steamed with black peppercorns. It is available at Italian markets.

1 tbs. butter
3 tbs. olive oil
4 chicken breasts, boned and skinned
½ lb. prosciuttini, chopped
2 tbs. flour

1 tbs. brandy
¼ cup white wine
3 tbs. chicken bouillon granules
juice from 1 lemon
2 tbs. chopped parsley

Place butter and olive oil in a large skillet over medium-high heat. When butter has melted, add chicken and brown well on all sides, about 10-12 minutes. Remove to platter and keep warm. Add prosciuttini to pan drippings. Stir in flour. Cook, stirring constantly for 1-2 minutes. Add brandy, wine, bouillon, lemon juice and parsley. Stir well. Return chicken to pan, coat with sauce and cook until heated through. Serve immediately.

Suggested Menu Plan First Course: Minestrone Genovese **or** Rigatoni with Red Peppers
Vegetable: Braised Fennel **or** Zucchini and Tomatoes with Herbs

Chicken Breasts Portieri

Very few ingredients go into this dish, but the result leads people to think otherwise. Chicken breasts are browned, combined with a Marsala sauce, smothered with mozzarella cheese and then baked.

6 chicken breasts, boned and skinned
½ cup flour
1 stick butter
3 tbs. olive oil
½ cup Marsala
½ cup water
1 large chicken bouillon cube
½ lb. mushrooms, sliced
½ lb. mozzarella, shredded

Coat chicken breasts with flour. Place butter and oil in a large skillet over medium heat. When butter has melted add chicken and cook until lightly browned, about 5-7 minutes. Remove from pan and arrange in baking dish. Pour Marsala into the skillet and stir to loosen browned bits. Add water and bouillon cube. Cook down until sauce thickens. Pour sauce over chicken. Layer mushrooms over sauce. Sprinkle shredded cheese over all. Bake at 450° for 10-15 minutes or until cheese is melted.

Suggested Menu Plan   First Course: Fresh Herb and Egg Soup **or** Risotto **or** Rice Pilaf

Vegetable: Broccoli with Garlic and Lemon **or** Braised Swiss Chard

Lemon Marinated Chicken

Chicken breasts are marinated in olive oil and lemon juice, breaded and cooked until golden brown. They can be served hot or cold.

4-6 chicken breasts, boned and skinned
¾ cup flour
salt and freshly ground pepper to taste
3 eggs
¾ cup seasoned bread crumbs
5 tbs. grated Parmesan cheese
¼ cup butter
2 tbs. olive oil
lemon wedges

Marinade
1 cup olive oil
juice of 1 lemon
¼ tsp. salt
¼ tsp. pepper

In a large bowl marinate chicken breasts in olive oil, lemon juice and salt and pepper for at least 1 hour, at room temperature. Mix flour, salt and pepper in a shallow bowl. Beat eggs lightly in a second bowl. Combine bread crumbs and Parmesan cheese in a third bowl. Shake excess marinade off chicken. Coat chicken first with flour, then with egg mixture and finally with bread crumb mixture. Warm butter and olive oil in a large skillet over medium-high heat. Add chicken and cook, turning once, until golden brown, about 4-5 minutes per side. Serve hot or cold with lemon wedges.

Suggested Menu Plan   First Course: Tortellini Soup **or** Tagiatelle Bolognese **or** Veal
and Porcini Mushrooms
Vegetable: Spinach and Prosciutto

Chicken with Balsamic Vinegar

The distinctive flavor of balsamic vinegar is used in this chicken dish. Sautéed chicken breasts are served atop a freshly made tomato sauce.

2 tbs. olive oil
6 tbs. butter
6 chicken breasts, boned and skinned
3 tbs. balsamic vinegar
salt and freshly ground pepper

Tomato Sauce
1 tbs. olive oil
1 onion, finely chopped
3 garlic cloves, minced
2 lbs. tomatoes, peeled, seeded and chopped
¼ cup tomato paste
½ tsp. sugar
salt and freshly ground pepper
2 (2 ozs. each) jars chopped pimientos
1 tbs. butter
garnish: chopped parsley

Heat olive oil and butter over medium-high heat in a large skillet. Add chicken and cook until lightly browned and tender, about 5-6 minutes each side. Transfer to heated platter and keep warm. Pour balsamic vinegar into the skillet and stir to loosen browned bits. Taste and adjust seasonings. Spoon some of hot tomato sauce on each plate. Top with chicken. Drizzle vinegar sauce over chicken. Sprinkle with parsley.

Tomato sauce: In a large saucepan heat olive oil over medium heat. Sauté onion and garlic for a few minutes. Add tomatoes, tomato paste, sugar, salt and pepper. Bring to a boil, reduce heat and simmer until very thick, about 50 minutes, stirring occasionally. Add pimientos and butter. Cook until heated through. Taste and adjust seasonings if necessary.

Suggested Menu Plan   First Course: Tuscan Bean Soup **or** Pesto over pasta
Vegetable: Asparagus with Parmesan Cheese

Chicken Cacciatore

Servings: 4

A hearty peasant chicken dish. Chicken is simmered in a robust tomato sauce with fresh vegetables, herbs and red wine.

1 chicken, cut into pieces
½ cup flour
2 tbs. butter
2 tbs. olive oil
salt and freshly ground pepper
   to taste
1 onion, thinly sliced
2 garlic cloves, minced
2 celery stalks, sliced

1 green pepper, cut into small pieces
1 cup sliced mushrooms
1 (28 ozs.) can Italian plum tomatoes
   with juice, crushed
½ cup red wine
3 tbs. fresh chopped basil
1 tsp. oregano
1 tsp. rosemary

Coat chicken with flour. Place butter and olive oil in a large skillet over medium heat. Add chicken pieces and brown well on all sides. Remove from pan and set aside. Season with salt and pepper. To drippings in skillet add onion, garlic, celery, green pepper and mushrooms. Cook until onions are soft and browned, about 10 minutes. Return chicken to skillet. Add crushed tomatoes with liquid, red wine, basil, oregano and rosemary. Bring to a boil, reduce heat, cover and simmer 45 minutes or until chicken is tender. Taste and adjust seasonings if necessary.

Suggested Menu Plan   First Course: Risotto **or** Potato Gnocchi.
A vegetable is not really needed, but you can serve Zucchini and Tomatoes with Herbs **or** Carrots with Gorgonzola **or** Braised Fennel after the main course

---

Chicken Fontina

Tender chicken bundles are stuffed with prosciutto and fontina cheese, breaded, baked and served with a brandy cream sauce.

8 chicken breasts, boned and skinned
8 slices fontina cheese, each slice ¼" thick and cut
   into 1"x2" rectangles
8 slices prosciutto
flour
3 eggs, well beaten
seasoned bread crumbs

salt to taste
1 stick butter
2 tbs. olive oil
3 tbs. brandy
2 tbs. flour
1 cup whipping cream

Pound chicken breasts to ¼" thickness. On each flattened piece lay a piece of cheese wrapped in a slice of prosciutto. Wrap chicken around packet, enclosing completely and securing with toothpicks. Place flour in shallow plate. Put beaten eggs in a second and bread crumbs in a third. Sprinkle chicken with salt and coat with flour, shaking off excess. Dip in beaten egg and finally in seasoned bread crumbs. In a large skillet over medium heat place 4 tbs. butter and olive oil. When butter has melted add rolls, cooking until browned evenly on all sides, about 15 minutes. Transfer rolls to ovenproof serving dish. Bake uncovered at 350° for 15 minutes. Meanwhile in same skillet over medium heat, loosen browned pieces from bottom of skillet. Add brandy and set aflame. When flame subsides, add remaining 4 tbs. butter. When melted, whisk in flour. Cook for 1 minute. Slowly whisk in cream, cooking and stirring until it boils and is thickened. Pour sauce over chicken and serve.

Suggested Menu Plan   First Course: Minestrone Soup **or** Minted Tomato Sauce over
pasta
Vegetable: Braised Swiss Chard

Peasant Chicken and Sausage

Italian sausage and chicken pieces are paired together for a hearty and satisfying dish.

2 red bell peppers
¼ cup olive oil
1 lb. sweet or spicy Italian sausage
  (or combination), cut into 1" pieces
6 chicken breasts,
  boned and skinned
4 garlic cloves, minced

½ cup dry white wine
½ cup chicken broth
1 tsp. rosemary
1 tsp. oregano
½ stick butter
salt and freshly ground pepper
  to taste

Char the peppers under a broiler until blackened on all sides. Place in a plastic bag and let stand 10 minutes. Peel and seed the peppers. Cut into thin strips. Heat oil in a large skillet over medium-high heat. Add sausage and cook until brown. Remove from pan and set aside. Cut chicken breasts into 1" pieces. Add to skillet and cook until done, about 5-7 minutes. Remove chicken from pan. Add garlic to skillet and sauté 2 minutes. Add wine and broth and bring to a boil. Add peppers, rosemary and oregano. Simmer about 10 minutes until thickened. Whisk in butter. Return sausage and chicken to skillet and heat through. Season with salt and pepper.

Suggested Menu Plan First Course: Spaghetti alla Carbonara **or** Fettucine with
Peas and Mushrooms **or** Polenta
Vegetable: Zucchini and Tomatoes with Herbs

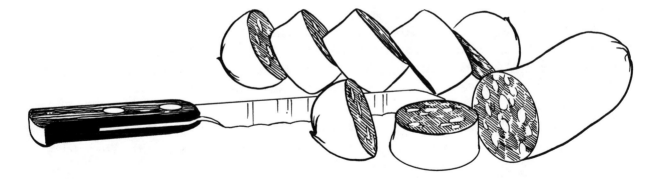

Chicken with Porcini Mushrooms

Wild dried Italian mushrooms have a wonderful woodsy, fragrant aroma. The liquid in which the mushrooms are reconstituted is full of flavor and should never be discarded.

1 tbs. olive oil
½ stick butter
4 chicken breasts, boned and skinned
¼ cup chopped parsley
1 chicken bouillon cube

¼ lb. prosciutto, diced
1 oz. porcini mushrooms, soaked in
    ¾ cup white wine
juice of ½ lemon

Warm olive oil and butter in a large skillet over medium heat. Add chicken breasts and brown on both sides. Remove from pan. Add parsley, bouillon cube and prosciutto. Cook until bouillon cube dissolves. Add mushrooms, wine and lemon juice. Return chicken breasts to skillet and simmer for 15 minutes or until chicken is tender. Pour sauce over chicken and serve.

Suggested Menu Plan First Course: Pasta with Sun-Dried Tomatoes **or** Pesto **or**
            Eggplant Rollettes
            Vegetable: Green Beans and Peppers with Tomatoes **or**
            Carrots with Gorgonzola

Chicken with Capers

Tender chicken breasts contrast nicely with the intense flavor of capers.

flour
salt and freshly ground pepper
4-6 chicken breasts, boned
  and skinned

1 stick butter
2 tbs. olive oil
juice of 1 lemon
1 tbs. capers, drained

Mix flour, salt and pepper together in a shallow dish. Coat chicken breasts with this seasoned flour, shaking off excess. Place butter and olive oil in a large skillet over medium heat. When butter has melted, add chicken breasts. Cook until they are golden brown on both sides, about 10-15 minutes. Remove to a platter and keep warm. To drippings in skillet, add lemon juice and capers. Stir well. Season with salt and pepper. Pour sauce over chicken and serve.

Suggested Menu Plan First Course: Bucatini with Broccoli **or** Penne Florentine **or** Risotto
Vegetable: Baked Eggplant

W/WINE

Stuffed Chicken Supremes

A tasty filling of Romano cheese, spinach, prosciutto, provolone and pine nuts is sandwiched between chicken breasts.

12 chicken breasts, skinned and boned
½ cup + 2 tbs. grated Romano cheese
1 cup cooked spinach, well drained
2 egg yolks
¼ tsp. nutmeg
½ tsp. salt
¼ tsp. freshly ground pepper
6 slices prosciutto
6 slices provolone cheese

2 tbs. pine nuts
flour
4 eggs, lightly beaten
seasoned bread crumbs
½ cup oil
6 tbs. butter
10 mushrooms, sliced
½ cup Marsala

Pound chicken breasts to ¼" thickness. Lay all 12 breasts on working surface. Sprinkle with ½ cup Romano cheese. Combine spinach, egg yolks, 2 tbs. Romano, nutmeg, salt and pepper in blender and puree. Spoon spinach mixture on each of six chicken breasts. Top with 1 slice each of prosciutto and provolone (cut to fit, if necessary) and 1 tsp. nuts. Cover each chicken breast and filling with another chicken breast. Gently pinch edges closed (use toothpicks if necessary; remove after baking). Dip chicken packets into flour, then beaten egg and finally bread crumbs. Pour oil into baking pan. Add chicken and turn to coat with oil. Bake 45 minutes at 400°, turning as needed for even browning. Remove carefully to serving platter and keep warm. Drain oil from pan leaving browned bits. Place pan over medium heat and add butter. Scrape up bits on bottom of pan. When butter has melted, add mushrooms and Marsala. Heat through, stirring constantly. Spoon over chicken and serve.

Suggested Menu Plan   First Course: Minestrone Soup **or** Pasta with Fresh Tomato
 Sauce **or** Eggplant Rollettes
 Vegetable: Broccoli with Garlic and Lemon **or** Braised Swiss
 Chard

Chicken with Garlic, Rosemary and White Wine

Servings: 4

A simple and tasty way of doing chicken breasts. They are pan-roasted with garlic, white wine, lemon juice and fragrant fresh rosemary.

2 tbs. butter
2 tbs. olive oil
3 garlic cloves, minced
4 chicken breasts, boned and skinned

1 tbs. fresh rosemary, minced
salt and freshly ground pepper to taste
½ cup white wine
juice of 1 lemon

Heat butter and oil in a large skillet over medium-high heat. Add garlic and chicken. Cook chicken until browned. Add rosemary, salt, pepper, wine and lemon juice. Allow wine to bubble rapidly for 2-3 minutes, and then lower the heat. Cover and simmer about 30 minutes or until chicken is done. Turn chicken once or twice while cooking. Transfer chicken to a serving platter. Boil down cooking juices and pour over chicken.

Suggested Menu Plan First Course: Escarole and Rice Soup **or** Farfalle with Chicken Livers
Vegetable: Peas with Pine Nuts **or** Spinach and Prosciutto

Fish and Shellfish

Seafood is an important part of the Italian's diet since the country is surrounded on three sides by water. With the exception of mountainous regions in the North and Umbria in Central Italy, all regions have access to the sea. The Adriatic and Mediterranean have an abundance of fresh fish and shellfish in all shapes, colors and textures. In addition the lakes of Lombardy and Veneto have a vast assortment of fish.

In this chapter, we've given you several ways to prepare fish which include poaching, baking, grilling and broiling. The sauces are kept simple and fresh vegetables and herbs are often added.

FISH AND SHELLFISH

Trout with Mushrooms and Artichoke Hearts

Servings: 6

Trout fillets are simmered in white wine, lemon juice and butter and served with a tasty sauce of mushrooms, artichoke hearts and capers.

2 ~~sticks~~ *TBSP. s* butter
½ cup white wine
juice from 2 lemons /
6 (8 ozs. each) trout fillets
salt and freshly ground pepper to taste

½ lb. fresh mushrooms, sliced
1 (14 ozs.) can artichoke hearts, sliced
2 tbs. capers, drained
garnish: chopped parsley

Melt butter in a large skillet over medium-high heat. Add wine and lemon juice. Bring to a boil. Add trout. Cover, reduce heat and simmer for about 15 minutes or until fish is done. Transfer fish to heated platter. Season with salt and pepper. Add mushrooms to liquid in skillet. Cook until mushrooms are soft and some of liquid has reduced. Add artichoke hearts and capers and cook for 3 minutes. Serve sauce over fish and garnish with chopped parsley.

Suggested Menu Plan   First Course: Fresh Herb and Egg Soup **or** Linguine with White Clam Sauce
Salad: Tomato and Basil Salad

Baked Sea Bass with Golden Raisins and Nuts

Servings: 4

Sea bass fillets are baked and then topped with golden raisins and crunchy nuts.

1½ lbs. sea bass filets
1 stick butter, melted
salt and freshly ground pepper to taste
juice of 1 lemon

⅓ cup pine nuts
2 tbs. butter
⅓ cup sliced almonds
⅓ cup golden raisins

Place sea bass in a baking dish. Brush with melted butter. Season with salt and pepper. Squeeze lemon juice over fillets. Bake at 400° 12-15 minutes or until fish is firm to the touch, yet flakes easily with a fork. While fish is cooking, place pine nuts in a small skillet over medium-low heat. Cook until lightly browned, about 3-4 minutes. Remove from pan. In same skillet melt 2 tbs. butter. Add sliced almonds and sauté until a pale gold color. Top fish fillets with nuts and raisins and serve immediately.

Suggested Menu Plan   First Course: Clam Chowder Soup **or** Risotto
Salad: Caesar Salad

Baked Fish with Fresh Tomatoes

Use any firm, white fish for this simple but tasty second course.

1 lb. fresh fish (cod, haddock, scrod)
3 cloves garlic, minced
paprika
¼ cup chopped fresh basil
salt and freshly ground pepper to taste

¼ cup olive oil
1 cup seasoned bread crumbs
¼ cup grated Parmesan cheese
2 tomatoes, sliced

Place fish in a single layer in a buttered baking dish. Sprinkle with garlic, paprika, basil, salt and pepper. Drizzle oil over fish. Top with bread crumbs and cheese. Arrange tomato slices on top. Bake at 375° for 35 minutes.

Suggested Menu Plan First Course: Scallops with Spinach Fettucine **or** Crab
Crespelle
Salad: Mushroom, Celery and Red Pepper Salad

Sole with Zucchini and Carrots

A delicate fish dish. Grated zucchini and carrots add color to this easy dish.

¼ cup dry vermouth
¼ cup water
juice of 1 lemon
1½ lbs. sole fillets
1 stick butter

1 onion, finely chopped
4 zucchini, coarsely grated
4 carrots, coarsely grated
3 tbs. minced fresh basil
salt and freshly ground pepper to taste

Pour vermouth, water and lemon juice into a large skillet. Bring to a boil. Reduce heat and add fillets in single layer in skillet. Cover and simmer 3-5 minutes, until fish just turns opaque. Transfer fish to a warm serving platter, reserving liquid. Add butter. When melted, add onion, zucchini and carrots. Cook over medium-high heat until vegetables are tender and some liquid has evaporated. Stir in basil and cook a few minutes. Season fish with salt and pepper. Pour vegetable mixture over fish and serve.

Suggested Menu Plan   First Course: Escarole and Rice Soup **or** Vermicelli with Crab
Salad: Cucumber Salad

Tuna with Lemon and Capers

Capers add zip to these pan-fried tuna steaks.

flour
salt and freshly ground pepper to taste
6 (8 ozs. each) 1" thick tuna steaks
4 tbs. butter

4 tbs. olive oil
juice of 2 lemons
½ cup minced parsley
½ cup capers, drained (or to taste)

Mix flour, salt and pepper together in a shallow dish. Coat tuna steaks with this seasoned flour, shaking off excess. Heat butter and olive oil in large skillet over medium heat. Add steaks in single layer. Cook about 8 minutes each side until golden brown and crusty. Remove to platter and keep warm. To drippings in skillet, add lemon juice, scraping up any browned bits. Add parsley and capers and heat through. Pour over fish and serve.

Suggested Menu Plan First Course: Linguine with White Clam Sauce **or** Crab
Crespelle
Salad: Warm Spinach and Basil Salad

Poached Halibut with Tomato Butter

A wonderful creamy tomato-butter sauce is served over poached halibut steaks.

6 medium tomatoes
2 lbs. halibut steaks
2 shallots, minced
salt and freshly ground pepper to taste
1 cup dry white wine
¾ cup heavy cream
2 sticks butter
pinch of cayenne pepper
garnish: 2 medium tomatoes, peeled, seeded and chopped
        2 tbs. chopped parsley

Chop tomatoes in a food processor. Strain juice from tomatoes into a medium saucepan. Discard pulp. Cook juice over medium heat until liquid reduces and thickens. Set aside. Place fish in a single layer in large skillet. Sprinkle with shallots, salt and pepper. Pour in wine, cover and bring to a boil over high heat.

Reduce heat and simmer 10 minutes or until fish is done. Transfer fish to a warm platter. Over medium heat, add tomato juice to skillet and reduce until it begins to thicken slightly. Add ¾ cup cream and continue to reduce. Whisk in butter, one small piece at a time. Add cayenne and taste for seasoning. Serve fish with sauce poured over the top and garnish with chopped tomatoes and parsley.

Suggested Menu Plan   First Course: Minestrone Soup **or** Risotto
Vegetable: Zucchini, Carrot and Fennel Salad

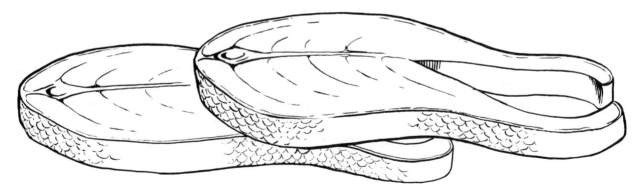

Stuffed Shrimp

Jumbo prawns are stuffed with bread crumbs, herbs and tiny shrimp and baked until golden.

4 tbs. butter
3 tbs. olive oil
1 medium onion, chopped
2 garlic cloves, minced
2 stalks celery, chopped
½ lb. tiny shrimp, uncooked
1 tsp. thyme
1 tsp. oregano

⅓ cup chopped parsley
½ cup white wine
6 tbs. tomato sauce
freshly ground pepper to taste
seasoned bread crumbs
18 jumbo shrimp, uncooked (8-10 per lb.)
melted butter

Place butter and olive oil in a large skillet over medium heat. When butter has melted, add onion, garlic and celery. Sauté until tender, but not brown. Add tiny shrimp and cook over low heat, about 5 minutes. Remove from heat. Stir in thyme, oregano, parsley, wine, tomato sauce, and pepper to taste. Add enough bread crumbs to make a stuffing mixture. Cook jumbo shrimp in boiling water just until they turn pink. Drain, cool and split, leaving shell intact. Stuff shrimp with stuffing mixture. Place on baking sheet. Drizzle with melted butter. Bake at 375° for 12-15 minutes. Serve with additional melted butter, if desired.

Suggested Menu Plan   First Course: Clam Chowder Soup **or** Pesto with Pasta
Salad: Warm Spinach and Basil Salad

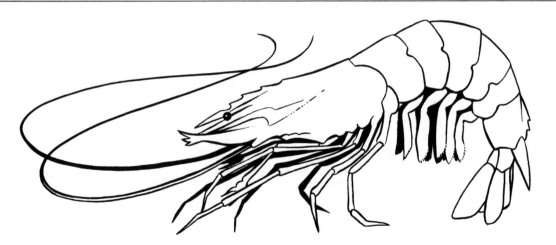

Shrimp Sautéed in Lemon and Garlic

Servings: 4

Scampi are quickly sautéed in a garlic-lemon butter for a classic Italian dish.

2 lbs. jumbo raw shrimp
2 sticks butter
2 tbs. olive oil
5-6 garlic cloves, minced
juice from 2 lemons

¼ cup white wine
grated rind from 1 lemon
½ tsp. (or more) red pepper flakes
⅓ cup chopped parsley
lemon wedges

Clean, shell and devein shrimp. Heat butter and olive oil in large skillet over medium heat. Add garlic and sauté for a few minutes. Add lemon juice and wine and cook until bubbly. Add shrimp and cook, stirring occasionally, until shrimp turns pink (about 3-5 minutes). Stir in lemon peel, pepper flakes and parsley. Serve hot with lemon wedges.

Suggested Menu Plan   First Course: Tuna Conchigle **or** Crab Crespelle
Salad: Caesar Salad

Brochettes of Marinated Shrimp

Servings: 6-8

Put your grill to use with these succulent basil-and-pancetta-wrapped marinated shrimp.

3 shallots, minced
3 garlic cloves, minced
¾ cup white wine
¾ cup virgin olive oil
3 tbs. white wine vinegar
juice from 1 lemon
¼ cup chopped fresh basil

¼ tsp. pepper
3 lbs. jumbo shrimp (about 30), shelled and deveined
30 fresh large basil leaves
30 thin slices of pancetta
10 bamboo skewers, soaked in water

Combine first 8 ingredients in large bowl. Stir in shrimp. Cover and refrigerate overnight. Drain shrimp and pat dry. Wrap each with basil leaf and then cover entirely with pancetta slice. Thread 3 shrimp through tail and head onto each skewer. Cover with plastic and refrigerate until ready to cook. Grill shrimp until just pink and opaque. Do not overcook. Serve hot.

Suggested Menu Plan   First Course: Seafood Stew **or** Pasta with Fresh Tomato
Sauce
Vegetable: Peas with Pine Nuts

Mussels and Clams fra Diavolo

Servings: 4

Mussels and clams float in a broth seasoned with onion, garlic, oregano, red pepper flakes and parsley.

3 dozen cherrystone **or** littleneck clams
3 dozen large mussels
1 cup water
4 tbs. butter
2 tbs. olive oil
1 onion, minced

2 garlic cloves, minced
1 tsp. oregano
½ tsp. red pepper flakes
¼ tsp. salt
⅓ cup chopped parsley
⅓ cup white wine

With stiff brush, scrub clams and mussels under cold running water to remove any sand; remove beards from mussels. Place water in large saucepan or Dutch oven over high heat. Bring to a boil and add clams. Reduce heat to medium-low, cover and cook until shells just open, about 6-8 minutes, stirring occasionally. With slotted spoon, remove clams to large bowl. To broth remaining in saucepan, add mussels and bring to a boil. Reduce heat to medium-low, cover and cook until shells open, about 6-8 minutes. stirring occasionally. Remove mussels from broth and add to clams.

Meanwhile in small saucepan over medium heat place butter and olive oil. When butter has melted add onion, garlic, oregano, red pepper flakes and salt. Cook until onion is tender. Add parsley and white wine and cook 2 minutes. Discard top shell from each clam and mussel; rinse clams and mussels on half shells in cooking broth to remove any sand. Let broth stand until sand settles to bottom. Carefully pour clear broth into a bowl; discard any sand. Return broth to saucepan, add wine mixture, clams and mussels. Warm over medium-high heat until heated through.

Suggested Menu Plan   First Course: Scallops with Green Fettucine **or** Risotto
Salad: Cucumber Salad

Swordfish with Roasted Pepper and Pine Nuts

Servings: 4

Grilled swordfish steaks are served with an unusual, light-tasting roasted red pepper and pine nut sauce.

3 large red peppers
¾ cup pine nuts, toasted
¼ cup balsamic vinegar
¾ cup extra virgin olive oil
1 tsp. salt

¼ tsp. freshly ground pepper
olive oil
salt and freshly ground pepper to taste
4 (8 ozs. each) 1" thick swordfish steaks

Char peppers in broiler until blackened on all sides. Place in plastic bag and let stand 10 minutes to steam. Peel, seed and cut into thin strips. Place in a large bowl. To toast pine nuts, place in small skillet over medium-low heat and cook until lightly browned. To red pepper strips add pine nuts, vinegar, olive oil, salt and pepper and mix well. Let sauce stand for 1 hour at room temperature. Brush steaks with olive oil and season with salt and pepper. Grill to desired doneness, about 3-4 minutes for very rare. Spoon sauce over cooked steaks.

Suggested Menu Plan   First Course: Any Gnocchi **or** Linguine with Clam Sauce
Salad: Mixed green salad with oil and vinegar

Vegetables

Agriculture is one of Italy's national resources. Vegetables are varied throughout Italy much like the climate. In the North, vegetables are grown such as turnips, potatoes, celery and mushrooms. In the mild and sunny regions, a wide variety of almost every type is grown. Tuscany is known for its beans, while Venetians have peas and asparagus. Tomatoes are grown throughout the country. They are used from an almost unripe green (Northern Italian salads) to a vibrant ripe red (Southern Italian sauces).

Italians prepare their vegetables very simply, perhaps served with only olive oil and lemon. Or, vegetables can be more elaborate dishes served as the main course in the evening.

Potatoes are a secondary vegetable in Italy, especially in the South. They are not served if pasta or rice precedes the main course.

The vegetables in this chapter are dishes to be served as an accompaniment to the meat, poultry or fish course.

VEGETABLES

Asparagus with Parmesan Cheese

Slender stalks of fresh asparagus are steamed until crisp-tender and then baked with freshly grated Parmesan cheese until golden. A specialty from Parma.

2 lbs. asparagus
½ tsp. salt
⅔ cup freshly grated Parmesan cheese
5 tbs. butter

Wash and trim the asparagus. Cook the asparagus in a microwave until crisp-tender. Or, bring water to a boil in a large skillet and cook the asparagus, uncovered, for 10-15 minutes. Smear the bottom of a rectangular bake-and-serve dish with butter. Arrange asparagus in the dish, side by side. Sprinkle with salt and grated cheese and dot with butter. Bake at 450° for about 15 minutes, until a lightly golden crust forms. Allow to settle a few minutes before serving.

Broccoli with Garlic and Lemon

Fresh broccoli is cooked until crisp-tender and then quickly sautéed in olive oil, fresh lemon juice and garlic.

1 large bunch broccoli (about 1½-2 lbs.)
4 tbs. olive oil
1 garlic clove, minced
juice of 1 lemon
salt and freshly ground pepper to taste

Separate broccoli florets. Peel stalks and slice thinly. Cook broccoli in boiling salted water until crisp-tender, about 5-7 minutes. Drain and set aside. Warm olive oil in a large skillet over medium heat. Add garlic and sauté until lightly golden. Add lemon juice, broccoli and salt and pepper. Cook for 2-3 minutes coating broccoli well. Serve hot.

Carrots with Gorgonzola

Diagonally sliced carrots are coated with melted Gorgonzola cheese for a delightful vegetable dish.

2 lbs. carrots, sliced diagonally
½ stick butter
4 ozs. crumbled Gorgonzola cheese
salt and freshly ground pepper to taste

Steam carrots until crisp-tender. Drain. Melt butter in a large skillet over low heat. Add cheese and cook until melted, stirring constantly. Add carrots and salt and pepper to taste. Cook until carrots are heated through and coated with cheese, stirring frequently. Serve hot.

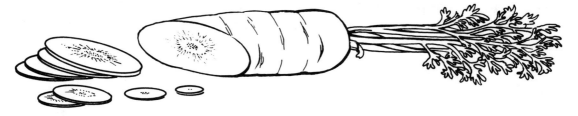

Braised Celery with Tomatoes

Servings: 4

Celery never tasted so good. Celery pieces are combined with onion, pancetta and Italian tomatoes and cooked until tender for a dish that will elicit seconds and thirds.

¼ cup olive oil
1½ cups thinly sliced onion
⅔ cup pancetta, cut into thin strips
1 lb. celery stalks, cut into 3" pieces
¾ cup Italian plum tomatoes, chopped
salt and freshly ground pepper to taste

Heat olive oil in a large skillet over medium-high heat. Add onion and sauté until very lightly browned. Add pancetta and cook 5 minutes. Add celery, tomatoes, salt and pepper. Blend well. Cover and cook over medium heat until celery is tender, about 25 minutes. If necessary, remove cover for the last few minutes to boil down the liquid. Serve hot.

Baked Eggplant

Buy eggplants that are good-sized, weighing about 1½ lbs. Look for ones with glossy, smooth skins. Eggplants should be resistant to the touch, never soft.

1 medium eggplant
½ cup butter
½ onion, finely chopped
¾ cup bread crumbs
2 eggs, beaten
½ tsp. salt
½ cup grated Parmesan cheese

Peel and cube eggplant. Boil until tender. Drain and mash with a fork. Melt butter in skillet and sauté onion over medium heat. Add ½ cup bread crumbs. Remove from heat and add eggs, salt and eggplant. Mix well and pour into buttered baking dish. Top with remaining ¼ cup bread crumbs, dot with butter and sprinkle grated cheese over top. Bake at 375° for 30 minutes. Serve.

Braised Fennel

Fennel, an important culinary ingredient in an ancient Roman kitchen, remains as popular with Italians today. It resembles celery in texture but with an anise or licorice taste.

4 heads fennel
1 tbs. salt
¼ cup butter
2 cups chicken broth

1 tbs. sugar
juice of 1 lemon
1 tsp. salt
½ tsp. freshly ground pepper

Cut tops off fennel. Chop feathery leaves and set aside. Cut fennel heads in half. Put them in a saucepan and cover with water. Add 1 tbs. salt and boil, uncovered, for about 15 minutes. Drain. Melt butter in a skillet. Add fennel, broth, sugar, lemon juice, 1 tsp. salt and pepper. Bring to a boil, lower heat, cover and simmer for about 30 minutes or until fennel is tender. Liquid can be thickened with a teaspoon of cornstarch or potato starch (dissolved in a tablespoon of water). Serve.

Green Beans and Peppers with Tomatoes

The excellent flavor of fresh green beans is brought out in this colorful vegetable dish.

1 lb. green beans
1 green pepper
¼ cup olive oil
1 onion, diced

1 cup coarsely chopped tomatoes
½ cup water
1½ tsp. salt
freshly ground pepper to taste

Snap ends off green beans. Slice green pepper. In a skillet, heat oil and sauté onion over medium heat, about 10 minutes. Add green pepper and tomatoes. Simmer about 25 minutes or until thickened. Add green beans. Stir well and add ½ cup water, salt and pepper. Cover and cook over low heat about 20 minutes or until beans are tender. Serve.

Baked Onions

Sweet tender onions bake under a crust of Romano and provolone cheese.

½ lb. shallots, peeled
1 whole head garlic, cloves
   separated and peeled
3 tbs. butter
3 tbs. olive oil
1 small onion, chopped
1 small carrot, chopped
1 tsp. thyme
1 tsp. crushed bay leaf
4 tbs. flour
2 cups milk

½ cup pureed tomatoes,
   fresh or canned
salt and freshly ground pepper to taste
3 tbs. butter
3 tbs. olive oil
2 red onions, sliced in ⅓" rings
1 yellow onion, sliced in ⅓" rings
¼ cup grated Romano cheese
¼ cup shredded provolone cheese
2 tbs. chopped fresh parsley

Blanch garlic and shallots separately in boiling, salted water just until tender. Drain and set aside. In large saucepan over medium heat place 3 tbs. butter and 3 tbs. olive oil. Add chopped onion, carrot, thyme and bay leaf. Cook until onion and carrot are tender, about 10 minutes. Remove from heat and stir in flour.

Return to heat and stir until mixture is golden, about 5 minutes. Whisk in milk gradually. Increase heat to high and bring to a boil, stirring constantly. Add tomato puree. Reduce heat and simmer 30 minutes, stirring occasionally. Season with salt and pepper.

Meanwhile place 3 tbs. butter and 3 tbs. olive oil in a large skillet over medium heat. Add sliced onions, blanched garlic, and shallots. Cover and cook over low heat until tender, about 25-30 minutes, stirring frequently. Add onion mixture to sauce, mixing well. Pour mixture into buttered shallow 2 quart baking dish. Top with cheeses. Bake at 350° until bubbly, about 30 minutes. Garnish with chopped parsley.

Peas with Pine Nuts

A tempting combination of fresh shelled peas, fresh rosemary and toasted pine nuts.

½ cup chicken broth
½ onion, chopped
½ tsp. sugar
3 lbs. fresh shelled peas
  (or 2-10 oz. pkgs. frozen, thawed)

3 tbs. olive oil
½ cup pine nuts
1 tbs. fresh minced rosemary
salt and freshly ground pepper to taste

In a medium saucepan combine broth, onion and sugar. Bring to a boil. Add peas. Simmer until tender, about 5-10 minutes. (If using frozen peas, cook for about 3 minutes.) Drain, discarding liquid and onion. Heat olive oil over medium heat in large skillet. Add pine nuts and stir until golden, about 3 minutes. Add rosemary and cook 1 minute. Add peas and cook until heated through. Season with salt and pepper. Serve hot.

Spinach and Prosciutto

Prosciutto, an unsmoked, salted and air-cured ham, is sautéed until crisp and then tossed with fresh steamed spinach.

2 lbs. spinach, stems removed
6 ozs. prosciutto, very thinly sliced
¼ cup olive oil
salt and freshly ground pepper to taste
lemon wedges

Blanch spinach in boiling, salted water for 2 minutes. Rinse with cold water, drain and pat dry. Separate prosciutto into meat and fat and cut into ⅛" dice. In a large skillet heat prosciutto fat and olive oil over low heat until fat is rendered and pieces are crisp, about 10 minutes. Remove browned pieces with slotted spoon and reserve. Mix in spinach, prosciutto meat, salt and pepper with drippings in skillet. Cover and cook until spinach is tender, about 8-10 minutes, adding water 2 tbs. at a time if it becomes too dry. Add reserved prosciutto fat and toss well. Serve hot. Pass lemon wedges separately.

Braised Swiss Chard

Prepare Swiss chard as you would spinach, but remove the coarse middle ribs before cooking.

2 lbs. Swiss chard
4 tbs. olive oil
4 tbs. butter
2 cups water
salt and freshly ground pepper to taste

Wash and tear chard into medium size pieces (2"), discarding middle ribs. Heat olive oil and butter in a large saucepan over medium-high heat. Increase heat to high and add Swiss chard. Mix well. Add water, salt and pepper. Cover and cook for about 7 minutes. Serve immediately.

Zucchini and Tomatoes with Herbs

Servings: 6

Zucchini is a favorite among Italian vegetables. Look for bright, glossy zucchini. Buy small ones, no longer than 6" and 1½" in diameter unless you are going to stuff them.

¼ cup olive oil
1 garlic clove, minced
1½ lbs. zucchini, thinly sliced
½ cup chopped onion
1 cup Italian plum tomatoes, chopped

¼ tsp. marjoram
1 tbs. chopped parsley
salt and freshly ground pepper
   to taste
2 tbs. grated Parmesan cheese

Heat 2 tbs. olive oil in a large skillet over medium heat. Add garlic and cook for 2 minutes. Add zucchini and cook until tender. In a saucepan, heat remaining olive oil over medium heat. Add onion and sauté about 5 minutes. Add tomatoes (with juice) and marjoram. Continue to cook about 20 minutes. Stir in parsley, salt and pepper. Coat the bottom of a casserole dish with a little olive oil. Spread half the zucchini in a layer on the bottom. Cover with half the tomato sauce and sprinkle with 1 tbs. cheese. Repeat the layering. Bake in a 400° oven for 20 minutes. Serve.

Salads

Nearly all Italian salads have a common dressing: olive oil, vinegar or lemon juice, salt and pepper. An herb or two may be added occasionally for variety. Although the proportions may vary, the ingredients remain constant.

Always use a top quality extra virgin olive oil which is from the first cold pressing of the olive. This is the purest, most flavorful oil. Italians never compliment the salad or the dressing but rather pay tribute to the olive oil.

The best vinegar to use is "aceto balsamico" or balsamic vinegar made in Modena in the Emilia-Romagna region of Northern Italy. It is the juice from the white trebbiano grape boiled down to a sweet syrup and then aged in a series of different wooden barrels. The process in which the wine yeasts turn the sugar to alcohol and then the acetic bacteria transforms it to acetic acid takes many, many years for this fine product.

Whether you serve a lettuce, mixed or single vegetable salad, always serve it *after* the main course. This is to cleanse the palate for the cheese, fruit or dessert course which follows. If served before, the taste of the vinegar would destroy the flavor of the wine which always accompanies the other courses.

SALADS

Warm Spinach and Basil Salad

Servings: 4-6

A wonderful warm dressing flavored with pine nuts and prosciutto coats fresh spinach and basil leaves.

6 cups fresh spinach leaves, washed
2 cups fresh basil leaves
½ cup virgin olive oil
3 cloves garlic, finely chopped

½ cup pine nuts
4 ozs. prosciutto, diced
salt and freshly ground pepper to taste
¾ cup freshly grated Parmesan cheese

Toss spinach and basil together in a large salad bowl. Heat oil in a skillet over medium heat. Add garlic and pine nuts. Sauté until nuts begin to brown slightly. Stir in prosciutto and cook another minute. Season to taste with salt and freshly ground pepper. Toss the salad with warm dressing and sprinkle with Parmesan cheese. Serve immediately.

Pear, Watercress and Potato Salad with Gorgonzola Cream Dressing

Servings: 4

This delicious blend of flavors makes an unusual salad.

2 cups watercress, stems trimmed
1 cup sliced boiled red potato
1 cup thinly sliced celery

2 ripe pears, thinly sliced
1/4 cup chopped toasted walnuts
1/4 cup crumbled Gorgonzola cheese

Place watercress on 4 salad plates. Toss potato and celery with a little dressing and place on watercress. Drizzle with remaining dressing and sprinkle with walnuts. Top with crumbled Gorgonzola.

DRESSING

3/4 cup olive oil
1/3 cup finely crumbled Gorgonzola
  cheese

1/3 cup heavy cream
2 tbs. fresh lemon juice
salt and freshly ground pepper

Process all ingredients in a food processor until blended.

Cucumber Salad

A Northern Italian salad with a dressing of sour cream.

4-5 cucumbers
1 cup sour cream
juice of 1 lemon
3 tbs. olive oil
3 tbs. chopped fresh parsley
salt and freshly ground pepper to taste

Peel cucumbers and slice into ¼" slices. Place in a large serving bowl. Combine remaining ingredients in small bowl and mix well. Mix with cucumber slices. Chill several hours to blend flavors. Serve at room temperature.

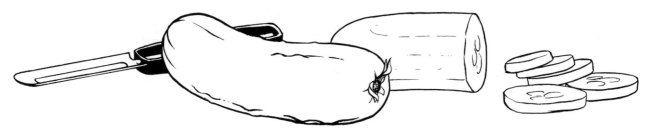

Tomato and Basil Salad

Servings: 6

Northern Italians usually prefer rather unripe tomatoes for their salads. Southern Italians use tender, sweet well-ripened tomatoes. Whichever you use, this is a basic Italian salad.

5 large firm tomatoes
salt and freshly ground pepper to taste
1 tbs. chopped fresh basil
⅓ cup olive oil
2 garlic cloves, minced

Cut tomatoes into thick slices and place on a serving platter. Mix remaining ingredients in a small bowl. When ready to serve, pour dressing over tomatoes.

Rice With Tomato and Cheese

Servings: 4-6

Rice salads are very popular in Italy in the summer. They can be varied by adding shellfish, ham, cheese or vegetables. Serve this salad as a light lunch or as part of an antipasto.

1½ cups raw rice
1¼ tsp. salt
3 tomatoes, cut in wedges
½ cup black olives, pitted and sliced
½ cup diced Swiss cheese

Dressing
2 tbs. red wine vinegar
juice of 1 lemon
1 tsp. Dijon mustard
½ tsp. marjoram
6 tbs. olive oil

Bring 3 cups of water to boil. Add rice and salt. Cover and simmer 15-20 minutes or until tender but firm. Drain and rinse with cold water. Place in large salad bowl. In a small bowl, combine all dressing ingredients except olive oil, and mix well. Whisk in oil. Add tomatoes, black olives and Swiss cheese to rice. Add dressing to rice and mix thoroughly. Serve chilled but not cold.

Zucchini, Carrot and Fennel Salad

A trio of vegetables is served with a dressing flavored with orange juice and walnuts.

3 zucchini, julienned
6 carrots, julienned
2 fennel bulbs, cored and sliced
lettuce leaves
1 orange, peeled and sliced

Dressing
⅓ cup orange juice
½ cup olive oil
3 tsp. fresh thyme
salt and freshly ground pepper to taste

Place vegetables in a large bowl. In a small bowl combine dressing ingredients. Pour over vegetables and toss. Place on lettuce-lined plates and garnish with orange slices.

Tuna and Bean Salad

Servings: 4

This is a salad from the Tuscany region. It makes a very nice second course for a summer meal or as part of a mixed antipasto.

1 cup dried white kidney **or** Great Northern beans
½ red onion, thinly sliced
1 (7 ozs.) can tuna fish in oil
salt and freshly ground pepper to taste
5 tbs. olive oil
2 tbs. red wine vinegar

Place beans in a large bowl. Cover with water and soak overnight. Drain and rinse. Place beans in a saucepan; cover with water, bring to a boil and simmer for 1 hour or until tender. Drain and let cool. Place in a salad bowl. Place onion in a small bowl and cover with cold water. Let stand 1 hour, changing water 2-3 times. Drain, pat dry and add to the beans. Drain oil from tuna, flake and add to salad. Add remaining ingredients. Toss gently and serve at room temperature.

Desserts

Italians do not place a great emphasis on desserts in their daily diet. They prefer the simplicity and beauty of fresh fruit served with a good cheese. When they do serve desserts, Italians prepare relatively simple mousses, custards, puddings and fresh or poached fruit served with a sauce.

Most Italians reserve the more elaborate desserts for special occasions such as religious holidays or family celebrations. They generally purchase fancy tarts and pastries, made by confectioners, for these special meals.

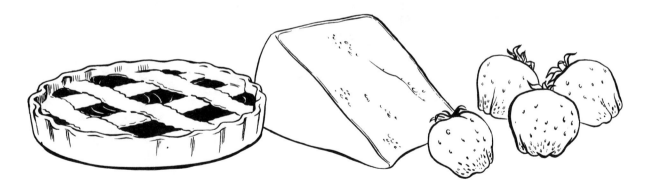

DESSERTS

Peaches Baked with Amaretti

Servings: 4

Halved juicy peaches are filled with crumbled amaretti biscuits, pine nuts, cocoa and Amaretto and then baked for a mouth-watering treat.

4 large ripe peaches
2 tbs. cocoa powder
5 amaretti biscuits, crumbled
2 egg yolks
2 tbs. Amaretto liqueur
2 tbs. pine nuts

Cut peaches in half and remove pits. Scoop out some of the flesh in middle of cavity to make room for filling. In a small bowl combine remaining ingredients, mixing well. Fill the peach cavities with this mixture. Grease a baking dish and place peaches in it. Bake at 400° for 15-20 minutes. Serve warm. Can also be served cold, but not directly from the refrigerator.

Tira Mi Su

In Italian, "Tira Mi Su" literally means "pick me up," and this easy dessert will!

1 lb. fresh mascarpone cheese (if unavailable, substitute 8 oz. each of whole milk ricotta and cream cheese)
1/4 cup sugar
1 tbs. brandy
31 ladyfingers
1 cup espresso coffee, cooled
1 recipe *Zabaglione*, page 161
fresh strawberries and raspberries for garnish
1-2 tbs. unsweetened cocoa for garnish

Prepare *Zabaglione* as directed and set aside. In a food processor, blend mascarpone, sugar and brandy until smooth. On a serving platter, arrange ladyfingers flat side up side by side. Moisten with 1/3 cup of coffee. Spread 1/3 of the cheese mixture over ladyfingers. Do this 2 more times, ending with cheese. Halve the remaining ladyfingers crosswide and make a fence around the cheese/ladyfinger layers. Pour *Zabaglione* over the cheese layers. Sprinkle with cocoa and add berries for garnish. Refrigerate until ready to serve.

Strawberry Frangelico

Servings: 6

This light summer dessert of ripe, red strawberries is sweetened with honey and Frangelico and topped with a drift of pink whipped cream.

3 baskets (pints) strawberries, hulled
3 tbs. honey
½ cup Frangelico liqueur
1 cup heavy cream

Reserve six of the ripest berries. Slice the remaining strawberries into large bowl. Add honey and liqueur, mixing lightly. Chill. In a medium bowl, beat cream until stiff. Puree reserved strawberries. Fold into whipped cream. To serve, place sliced strawberries in serving bowl or individual dishes. Top with pink whipped cream.

Cointreau Oranges

Orange slices are sprinkled with walnuts and topped with a Cointreau-flavored sauce.

peel from 1 orange, thinly sliced
6 large oranges
½ cup walnuts, chopped
2 tbs. butter

⅓ cup sugar
¼ cup Cointreau
juice of 1 orange

Bring some water to boil in a small saucepan. Add sliced orange peel and boil 5 minutes to reduce bitterness. Drain and dry well. Peel six oranges, making sure to remove all the white membrane. Cut into slices about ⅓" thick. Remove seeds. Arrange slices, slightly overlapping, on individual plates (or one large platter). Sprinkle with walnuts. Melt butter in a small saucepan over medium heat. Stir in sugar, orange peel and Cointreau. Stir until sugar is dissolved. Add orange juice. Cook, stirring occasionally, until sauce is of medium-thick consistency. Spoon over oranges and serve.

Coffee Cream Mousse

Coffee, brown sugar, cinnamon and brandy flavor this light and airy frozen mousse. Toasted pine nuts add crunch.

4 egg whites
¼ cup sugar
½ cup heavy cream
2 egg yolks
2 tbs. firmly packed brown sugar
1 tsp. cinnamon

1½ tsp. instant coffee crystals
  dissolved in 1 tsp. hot water
2 tbs. brandy
pinch salt
¼ cup pine nuts, toasted

In a large bowl, beat egg whites until frothy. Gradually add sugar and continue beating until stiff peaks form. In a medium bowl, beat cream until thick. Combine yolks, brown sugar, cinnamon, instant coffee, brandy and salt in another large bowl. Beat with electric mixer until light in color and thick. Carefully fold in egg whites and cream just until blended. Some streaks of white may remain. To toast pine nuts, place in a small skillet and cook over medium-low heat until lightly browned, about 5 minutes. Spoon ⅓ cup of coffee cream into each of 4 dessert glasses. Sprinkle each with 1½ tsp. pine nuts. Cover tightly and freeze until firm. Let stand in refrigerator one hour before serving.

Lemon Mousse

A light and elegant finish to an Italian meal. Fresh squeezed lemon juice and grated lemon rind give tartness to this refreshing mousse.

1 envelope unflavored gelatin
2 tbs. white wine
⅓ cup fresh lemon juice
2 tbs. grated lemon rind

3 eggs, separated, plus 1 egg white
⅓ cup + 2 tbs. sugar
1 cup heavy cream, whipped
slices of lemon or fresh mint for garnish

Sprinkle gelatin over wine in top of double boiler and let soften 5 minutes. Add lemon juice and rind and stir the mixture over hot water until gelatin is dissolved. In a large bowl, beat egg yolks with 2 tbs. sugar. Gradually beat in the gelatin mixture. Fold in whipped cream. In another large bowl, beat 4 egg whites until foamy, and then add ⅓ cup sugar and beat to soft peaks. Fold one-fourth of the egg white mixture into cream mixture. Add cream mixture to the remaining egg whites and fold gently until combined. Spoon into stemmed glasses and chill for several hours. Garnish with lemon slices or fresh mint.

Zabaglione with Fresh Fruit

The classic Italian dessert. Egg yolks, sugar and Marsala wine are whipped into a thick, golden pudding in about 6 minutes. Here we serve it over fresh fruit.

4 egg yolks
¼ cup sugar
½ cup Marsala wine
fresh fruit

Place egg yolks and sugar in a large metal bowl or the top of a double boiler. Whip with a wire whisk (or electric mixer) until pale yellow and creamy. Place bowl over boiling water. Add Marsala slowly and continue beating. The zabaglione is ready when it triples in volume and forms soft mounds, about 4-6 minutes. Spoon over fresh fruit or serve alone in goblets.

Chocolate Custard with
Champagne Zabaglione

Molded chocolate custards with cinnamon and brandy are smothered in a creamy champagne zabaglione sauce.

Chocolate Custard
2 cups heavy cream
1 cinnamon stick
8 egg yolks
⅓ cup sugar
1 tbs. brandy
1 tsp. vanilla
4 ozs. semisweet chocolate, finely chopped

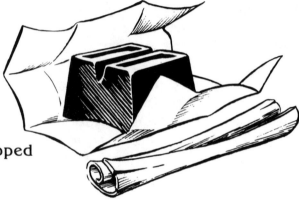

Champagne Zabaglione
½ cup champagne
⅓ cup sugar
4 egg yolks
½ cup heavy cream

Chocolate custard: In a medium saucepan, bring cream and cinnamon stick to a simmer. In a large bowl beat egg yolks, sugar, brandy and vanilla until pale yellow and ribbons form when beaters are lifted. Beat ½ cup of the hot cream into the yolk mixture. Stir chocolate into the remaining hot cream and then whisk into the yolk mixture. Discard the cinnamon stick. Pour into 8 lightly oiled custard cups. Set custard cups in a pan of hot water and bake in a 325° oven about 30 minutes, or until a knife inserted in the center comes out clean. Let stand at room temperature for 30 minutes. Cover and refrigerate at least 4 hours. Unmold onto a plate and spoon zabaglione over the custards.

Champagne zabaglione: Combine champagne, sugar and yolks in a metal bowl or top of double boiler. Set over simmering water and whisk until mixture mounds when spooned, about 8 minutes. Set bowl in ice and beat until cool. In another bowl, beat the cream to soft peaks. Fold into the zabaglione. (Can be prepared up to 2 hours ahead.)

Ricotta Pudding with
Amaretto Sauce

A pudding made with sweet ricotta cheese and served with a warm Amaretto-flavored sauce.

Pudding
1 lb. ricotta cheese
⅓ cup sugar
3 eggs
1 egg, separated
3 tbs. bread crumbs
2 tbs. flour
1 tsp. almond extract
2 tsp. grated lemon rind

Amaretto Sauce
1½ cups water
3 tbs. sugar
1 tbs. lemon juice
¾ cup Amaretto liqueur
3 tbs. cornstarch
¼ cup butter

Pudding: Butter an 8" souffle dish. Coat with sugar, shaking out excess. In a large bowl combine ricotta, sugar, 3 eggs and 1 egg yolk, bread crumbs, flour, almond extract and lemon rind. Beat with electric mixer until well blended. In another bowl beat remaining egg white until stiff but not dry. Fold into ricotta mixture. Pour into prepared dish and bake at 375° for 40-45 minutes or until lightly browned and edges begin to pull away from dish. Spoon into dessert dishes and top with warm Amaretto sauce.

Amaretto sauce: Combine water, sugar and lemon juice in a small saucepan. Bring to a boil. In a small bowl mix Amaretto and cornstarch until smooth. Blend into sugar mixture. Cook over medium-low heat until thickened and smooth, stirring occasionally. Blend in butter. Serve warm. Makes 2½ cups.

Amaretto Chiffon Cheesecake

Servings: 10

A fluffy chiffon cheesecake sits atop a crust made with amaretti cookies with an added surprise of melted chocolate spread over the crust.

Crust
1¼ cups crumbs from amaretti cookies
½ stick unsalted butter, softened
2 ozs. semisweet chocolate, chopped

Filling
16 ozs. cream cheese, room
   temperature
½ cup Amaretto liqueur
1 envelope unflavored gelatin
¾ cup water
3 eggs, separated
¾ cup sugar

2 tsp. finely grated orange rind
2 tsp. finely grated lemon rind
pinch of salt
1 cup heavy cream
garnish: ¾ cup heavy cream, whipped
   and sweetened with 3 tbs. confectioners
   sugar, 1 tbs. amaretti crumbs

Crust: In a food processor, combine cookie crumbs and butter. Press onto the bottom of a 9″ springform pan. Bake in a 350° oven for 10-12 minutes, or until lightly browned. Place chopped chocolate on the hot crust. After a few minutes, spread melted chocolate evenly over crust. Chill until ready to fill.

Filling: In a large bowl beat cream cheese with an electric mixer (or in a food processor) until very smooth. Gradually beat in Amaretto. Set aside. Sprinkle gelatin over ¼ cup cold water to soften. Let stand 5 minutes. Beat yolks lightly in a small saucepan. Stir in remaining ½ cup water and ½ cup sugar and stir constantly over moderate heat just until the mixture coats a spoon. Remove from heat, add softened gelatin mixture and stir until dissolved. Gradually beat the warm yolk mixture into the cream cheese mixture. Stir in orange and lemon rind. Cool completely to room temperature.

In a large bowl whip egg whites with salt to soft peaks. Add remaining ¼ cup sugar. In another bowl, whip cream to soft peaks. Gradually fold egg whites and whipped cream into cream cheese mixture. Pour the filling over the crust. Refrigerate at least 6 hours. Garnish with additional whipped cream and amaretti cookie crumbs.

INDEX

SERVE CREATIVE, EASY, NUTRITIOUS MEALS WITH NITTY GRITTY® COOKBOOKS

The Versatile Rice Cooker
The Dehydrator Cookbook
Waffles
The Coffee Book
The Bread Machine Cookbook
The Bread Machine Cookbook II
The Bread Machine Cookbook III
The Bread Machine Cookbook IV
The Sandwich Maker Cookbook
The Juicer Book
The Juicer Book II
Bread Baking (traditional), revised
The Kid's Cookbook, revised
The Kid's Microwave Cookbook
15-Minute Meals for 1 or 2
Recipes for the 9x13 Pan

Chocolate Cherry Tortes and Other Lowfat Delights
Lowfat American Favorites
Lowfat International Cuisine
The Hunk Cookbook
Now That's Italian!
Fabulous Fiber Cookery
Low Salt, Low Sugar, Low Fat Desserts
What's for Breakfast?
Healthy Cooking on the Run
Healthy Snacks for Kids
Creative Soups & Salads
Quick & Easy Pasta Recipes, revised
Muffins, Nut Breads and More
The Barbecue Book

The Wok
New Ways with Your Wok
Quiche & Soufflé Cookbook
Cooking for 1 or 2
Meals in Minutes
New Ways to Enjoy Chicken
Favorite Seafood Recipes
No Salt, No Sugar, No Fat Cookbook
New International Fondue Cookbook
Extra-Special Crockery Pot Recipes
Favorite Cookie Recipes
Authentic Mexican Cooking
Fisherman's Wharf Cookbook
The Creative Lunch Box

Write or call for our free catalog.
Bristol Publishing Enterprises, Inc.
P.O. Box 1737, San Leandro, CA 94577
(800)346-4889; in California (510)895-4461